SINGING ALL THE VERSES

Essays from a Mid-American

PEG GUILFOYLE

Also by Peg Guilfoyle

"Arts Roots in Saint Paul: The Seventies! "
The Saint Paul Almanac, Volume 12

*The Condons and the Gradys Before 1911:
History, Essay, and Genealogy*

"Uncle Tex's Wedding"
The Saint Paul Almanac, Volume 11

*The Van Wagners in America 1637-1943:
History, Essay, and Genealogy*

Offstage Voices: Life in Twin Cities Theater
Minnesota Historical Society Press

The Guthrie Theater: Images, History, and Inside Stories
Nodin Press

The Basilica of Saint Mary: Voices From A Landmark

also books produced on commission for private and
corporate clients

Peg Guilfoyle | Peg Projects, Inc.
pegguilfoyle.com

For, and to, my family and friends.

Every book is, in an intimate sense,
a circular letter to the friends of him who writes it.

Robert Louis Stevenson

Singing All The Verses

Peg, age 9

CONTENTS

FOREWORD

This book has been cooking for a long time. Some portions appeared before in some form, in newspapers and periodicals, or as radio commentary. The Guthrie pieces are excerpted from my Guthrie Theater book. *Wooden Horses* is an excerpt from an unpublished book manuscript. The final piece was delivered as a speech. Most of these I've left just as they were when I wrote them. I've gathered them by a kind of alchemical process from my files; do they, I asked myself, still seem to have heat?

The larger part is new to print, whether long-simmering or sudden. Several are freshly-minted, just for this book.

I want to thank my children and husband who, sometimes unknowingly, have provided content over time. My siblings, too, and my ancestors, particularly my beautiful mother. They all populate these pages; the pages, though, are mine. Thanks also to my many colleagues, communities, friends, and virtual sisters and brothers. All readers and enthusiasts, thank you. I've been listening hard the whole time.

Peg Guilfoyle

2020

INTRODUCTION

This book was named *Singing All the Verses* long before it was written. In a telling commentary on my writing life, either sad or laudatory, I have manuscript notes going back ten years, noting what pieces should be in and out, and a long, long list of work I just haven't gotten to writing yet. When some of the clamor of daily life abated and this book rose to the top of my hot list, I laid out all those manuscripts and notes on the big dining table and passed my hands over them, trying to see which ideas and squibs had life in them. The ones here are some that still leapt at me. Many more are crowding behind them. Every week, I see something that blazes up in me a flash of impulse. *That's* interesting, I think. I'd like to look at that.

At my church (Unitarian Universalist and sorry, Father O'Mara), the admirable music directors have a particular view about hymn singing. In my childhood church, where I was a preteen organist at the early Mass on Sundays, I was directed to lead the congregation in by playing the last two phrases of the chorus, then they would sing one verse, repeat the chorus, and done. Speedy Masses were desirable; singing together was just a component, not an anchor. The singing was often anemic, and I never did learn how to operate the foot pedals to deepen the tone. My organ sound was thin and reedy, but I loved the quiet of the early-morning church and the way the light fell in from the east.

The UUs, though, sing all the verses. I don't know if it's a policy or a principle or just a habit; I don't know if it's specific to our congregation or a universal approach. What I do know is that it reveals a truth I never noticed. It is partly a matter of momentum; the music itself gathers power as it continues and extends. And often the beauty and power and sweep of sacred singing is contained in the later verses. The words carry the meaning, which is, after all, the point of sacred singing. The first verse is just a scene setter. If you want to dive deep, you sing them all.

Amazing grace! How sweet the sound
That saved a wretch like me!
I once was lost, but now am found,
Was blind, but now I see.

'Twas grace that taught my heart to fear,
And grace my fears relieved;
How precious did that grace appear

The hour I first believed.

Through many dangers, toils, and snares,
I have already come;
'tis grace that brought me safe thus far,
and grace will lead me home.

When we've been there ten thousand years,
Bright shining as the sun,
We've no less days to sing God's praise
Than when we'd first begun.

I have long been a person who sings all the verses. I was a child from a family dominated by a substance-abusing, and abusive, father and a mother who bent all her powers to keep that secret unexamined and ignored. I found schooling easy, a respite from the cacophony of home life as a young child and a complete escape as a young woman. I was intrigued by its variety—astronomy (could a girl be an astronomer?) and film studies (so different from dates to the movies) and piano studies (but five hours per day in the practice room excluded too much).

As a student at Indiana University, the biggest protest march I ever saw was against a tuition increase. I taught horseback riding for the university, both forward seat and saddle seat, and was thrown out of the barn when one of the stallions was put to stud. "You can't watch this," said the reigning cowboy, who was also the reining cowboy. I don't think my interest was prurient, but I'm sure his decision was.

My roommates, all from Indiana, moved out of the dorm for our junior year. "Where does she *go?*" they soon began asking each other of my absences to the barn or to the theater's green room.

I took an apartment alone in senior year, and received two proposals of marriage, one with a big diamond that would have required me to move to North Dakota. I gave it back. I dated a predental student who was cute and smart and funny. Having been the victim of painful dental work by a dentist whom my father said was cheaper, I dropped the student the day after he came over to show me his gleaming pack of dental tools and admiringly spread them out on the kitchen table.

Actually, I gave him to my ex-roommate.

The day after I graduated, I started work in the theater, a wonderful life for a generalist and a person who loves problems, since each play presents an endless series of problems to be solved. The rehearsal room is an absorbing crucible, and out of it must spring a believable universe. Creators have to live in that universe in order to make a complete world for the audience.

I added arts management to my skill set when I started managing a burgeoning program of poets and painters and musicians. There I learned something about the powerful lure of all the arts, a permanent life lesson and inoculation against intellectual boredom.

In my twenties, I traveled and worked in the west (summer stock with the stars, historic stages and their auras, stagehands and beer and barbecues, and the occasional actor fling), the southwest (saguaros and ocotillos, desert sunsets, the pleasures of warm winters), and Chicago (guesting in a palatial northside apartment, late-night cabs, the buzz of downtown sidewalks). I spent a summer as a youth worker in a north-woods camp and drove a van full of rural teenagers to a Fourth of July powwow, where they saw so many Native Americans they were afraid to get out of the car. And I traveled one sunny, long-day summer in Alaska, hiking the Chilkoot Trail, canoeing on the Yukon River, once carrying a heavy pack up a rock bowl in a heavy wind and impulsively leaning back. The wind supported me. When a grizzly bear appeared suddenly in heavy brush, my companion declared: "The bear bells aren't working. I want to go home."

In my thirties, I brought my vagabond dog home to

Minnesota and started ten years of production management work at the Guthrie, the place that taught me everything I know about standards and work ethic. It was a golden time there and then, full of ambition and caprice and high invention. The people were the best in their field, and I was the best in mine. I married outside the profession and had a child. With my second, I could no longer give either of my loves—the work and the family—everything I had. With pain and regret and relief, I stopped. When the boss asked what I wanted for my farewell party—we were all big on parties—I said, "will there be champagne?" And there was.

We lived on a hobby farm way outside the city, with grand, mature trees and a farmhouse I loved, where my husband could step outside to call the dogs *sans* pants and my little ones could be perched horseback from a young age. I put in a field of wildflowers and threw a massive holiday party every year, with sledding in the pasture. Our family watched the Perseids meteor showers, Comet Kohoutek, and satellites passing overhead; migrating monarchs always stopped in our side yard. I became the consummate school volunteer and sat nine years on the board. I adored those years with my children.

It occurs to me that this has not been a focused life, unfolding in a straight line.

I have always been interested in everything, and my passionate interests are retained as currents in the big stream. I can dip my cup in anywhere and feel my love for a darkened empty stage with just a ghost light burning or a young poet leaning in to talk with a child. A golden eagle on the bank of the Yukon as our canoe was carried swiftly past. My mother dancing around a campfire on a Michigan beach.

Singing justice songs and old-time religious songs in a free-harmony group begun to attend a friend in the last year of her life. We sang; she sang. Eventually we formed a circle of chairs at her memorial service and left one empty, adorned with her favorite hat.

Finding a displaced church angel for sale in an antique shop and carefully carrying her home. Or is it a him? Angel gender is fluid.

Singing in the gospel choir in a modest church basement, providing syncopation and backup to a soaring and improvising tenor, wishing sometimes to be on the sidewalk outside to hear the power emanating from those basement windows, and then overjoyed to be in the room and in the chorus. "I'm doing the best I can with what I got," we sang.

My theater years created in me an unyielding episodic rhythm. It's simple and predictable. A title is chosen, cast, designed, rehearsed. It opens in a frenzy of concentration that shuts out everything else. It plays, and then comes closing night. It's irretrievably gone; sometimes the physical show goes literally into the dumpster. There is a moment to breathe; then comes another project.

Pieces of writing are projects, too: utterly engrossing. Getting lost in the research is not a risk or a detour; it's a pleasure. You don't really want to do anything else but read more deeply and search more strongly for the traces of your ancestors in famine Ireland, until you think you can glimpse them in that terrible landscape, moving toward Cobh and boarding a ship. And then you write that book, and it's done.

When you leap from one happy vortex to another, it is possible to live long years without raising your head to look at the longer threads of your life. This book is a way of looking.

The things I have loved, I have loved long. And they do weave together into a life.

I remember bad things, too, but I give them short shrift.

Years ago, I read Tillie Olsen's seminal work on writers, *Silences*, and then fled her premise that writers let other things get in the way of their voices, sometimes for years and sometimes forever. My flight was, I'm sure, based both on uneasy recognition and fear. Aversion. What she described has happened to me. The impulse has never stopped, and I have written a lot over the years. But I have never written my story, my own song. That has been the verse unsung.

Some people find a single passion and stick with only that for their whole lives. These are single-minded people who rise to the top of their professions and stay there, who give up everything else to pursue their one ideal, who don't seem to care about much else.

I do not understand these people. The world is an enormous, expansive buffet. How can one eat from just one part of the table?

Ours is a world of wonders. Every glimpse full of astonishing detail. Every verse worth singing individually.

We join our voices to many others, singing as a big, booming chorus and sometimes closing our eyes. There are changes of key and a long, strong closing. The chord resolves into a fervent and tranquil amen.

Verse I

LOOKING AT THE ARTS

Quarantine Music, *Andante* But Not *Agitato*

A few years ago, I was ambling through one of those antique stores composed of bookshelves, tables of different heights, glassed-in display cases with peculiar locks, and usually a section of wall with a display of prints, mounted paper ephemera, and a moose head mount. My husband and I do this browsing for relaxation, everywhere we go. We've spent many quiet hours perusing the detritus of lives unseen, objects now separated from their *manna*—that is, whatever power they once retained in the context of their bygone humans. Without their people, most of these objects seem a little reduced, a little dusty, a little lost. Look at this, we'll say to each other. I've never seen one like this, one of us will say. Occasionally, we pick something up and bring it home.

That is how I came by my present quarantine companion, *A Treasury of Grand Opera*, published in 1946 by Simon and Schuster. As soon as I saw it sitting on a table amid some undistinguished pottery and a bowl of key chains, I knew it was mine. Oversized, soft-covered, the book's front and back are both adorned with simple watercolors of famous opera moments—Carmen shaking her tambourine, Aida reclining in a sultry pose, both characters with mouths open in song. That must be Mephistopheles in the red with the dramatic posture, sweeping his cape over his face. Only a little water-stained, in good shape really, and inside, the book contains four-hundred-and-four slightly tattered pages of production histories, vignettes, musical descriptions, and marvelous details. The principal characters of each opera are listed, the *mise en scène* described, the first performance date and location noted. And the chorus parts are also listed: for *Carmen*, I did not remember that the company is filled out with "dragoons, gypsies, smugglers, cigarette girls, officials and urchins."

The core of the book, and its chief appeal to me, lies in page after page of piano scores for *Don Giovanni*, *Lohengrin*, *La Traviata*, *Faust*, *Aida*, *Carmen*, and *Pagliacci*. Suddenly, my largely empty apartment with a piano seems like an advantage. Be gone to my customary desultory fiddlings at the keyboard. Grand opera awaits. There is room for me amid the gypsies, urchins, and cigarette girls, and no one will know if I attempt the arias. I am all alone.

All this for five dollars. That is the same price the book sold for in 1946, but it is a steep discount when you consider the different value of the dollar. Five dollars in 1946 is the equivalent, I read, of $66 today. Bargain! This is the way you learn to think after a few decades of wandering the antique shops of the land.

And that is how I, in the time of coronavirus, have come to sit every day at my vintage upright piano, picking out the simplified arrangements of the great arias and filling in around them with a grand and complete orchestra in my head. *Ridi, Pagliacco!* I warble and give it a good slowdown, a *molto ritard* as the score indicates, as my avatar tenor throws his head up toward the hard-edged follow spot and lets his shoulders droop in the harlequin costume. "Laugh then, Pagliacco, for the love that is dying. Laugh through the pain that is destroying your heart!", he sings. "Full-voiced to the breaking point," says the score. "Expressively." And, just before the final note, "sobbing."

Good thing my husband is not at home when I play this. Good thing the apartment building has concrete walls.

I warble in English; my Italian is limited, if enthusiastic. I've picked my Italian up mostly from the subtitles of Metropolitan Opera broadcasts, which makes my vocabulary emphatic but not extensive. *Coraggio!* I can cry, which means *Courage!* I can also exclaim in Italian "death", "blood", "kill", and "vengeance". In amorous vein I may say *amore,* that is, love both as a noun and a form of address, male and female. *Cara,* I say, or *Caro!* Dear, embrace me! Grand opera nearly always includes entreaty and penitence, and so I recognize "heavenly father" and "eternity" and "sin". All of these words, plus contextual clues from staging, lights, and costumes -- the *mise en scène* -- enable me to understand most of the plots in grand opera. They do not make me a good conversationalist.

Being a person who is always interested in the backstory, I was rather hoping that *Treasury* editor Henry W. Simon would prove to be related to publisher Simon and Schuster, perhaps a disreputable cousin paid to stay offshore after some disgraceful episode, then falling in love with the Opera from a garret in Venice, just down the *campo* from Teatro La Fenice. Sad to say, not the case. But editor Mr. Simon tells a bit of his own story in the introduction to the collection. He writes:

"A Christmas present received over thirty years ago [that would make it before 1916, dear reader] is indirectly responsible for this book. It was a small badly bound collection of dreadfully simplified piano arrangements of the principal arias from several grand operas... Despite its

19

palpable inadequacies, that little book inspired in my adolescent breast a love for grand opera that is today strong as ever. I played and read it through to pieces."

I love these little glimpses into the backstory, why people are inspired to make something, and the travels these things subsequently make. My 1946 score is a direct descendant of that 1916 collection; I am working my way through it in 2020. I am quite considerably beyond adolescence, but I am as enthralled as young Henry likely was. Henry Simon died in 1970. I picked up the score in that dusty jumble shop some forty years after his death, and more than sixty after its publication. Where was it in the meantime?

I have always loved sight-reading at the piano. I used to think this kind of brain exercise would stave off dementia, until a more musically literate and more worried-about-that friend told me it was memorizing, not sight-reading, that was useful. I still like sight-reading. It engages all of my attention, most of my senses, and some of my motor skills. I do not think about anything else while I'm playing through *A Treasury of Grand Opera*. I am not troubled by my mistakes or the awkward pauses when it's time to turn the pages in a 404-page perfect-bound volume, which is actively trying to return to its closed state. A human page-turner, even if I had one, would defeat the purpose of free fumbling, and might disturb the mighty imaginary orchestra surrounding me at the piano.

Reading music is reading a foreign language, really, which I learned to understand in piano lessons that started in second grade. Thank you, Mrs. Salter. I am far from fluent now, but when I lay out a score on a tall table and page through it, I can feel my brain changing, knowing that I am seeing and hearing something that is blank to many people. It's like a door that I know how to walk through. And on the other side is a breeze. When I set that score on the piano and my fingers on the keys, I feel it blowing.

I do not, however, seek humiliation. Therefore, I do not sight-read and play anything marked *presto* (at a rapid tempo) or even *allegretto* (fairly briskly) or, heaven forbid, *agitato* (to play quickly, with agitation and excitement). I am an *andante* player, which means a tempo that has something to do with walking, which I think of as related to rhythmic ease and steadiness and grace. It does not mean hurry. It does not mean "look out, here comes a complicated key change" or a series of sixteenth notes that blacken the staff or a sudden 9/8-time signature. *Andante* has something to do with heartbeat and with strength and communion, rather like the feeling of stepping into a choir and joining your voice to that of others. It gives permission to pause, looking ahead, and to simplify that left hand from rolling chords to a series of uncomplicated octaves. *Andante* allows space to hear the melody and to make it sing above the accompaniment.

And *andante* is within my skill range, my range of right now. I turned away from serious piano study, and serious piano practice, when I first went to university and discovered that I really didn't want to spend five hours a day in a practice room. It was, after all, 1968. People were marching across campus protesting and shouting and I was, for the first time, beginning to listen. I still have the sheet music for my freshman-year showpiece, the Brahms Rhapsody Opus 79 No. 2, and it is marked up with fingerings and notes and my dormitory room address. My hands still remember some of it. It is marked *molto passionato, ma non troppo allegro*. Very passionately, fast but not too fast. I have a dream that someday I'll pick up the Brahms again, playing it passionately, but not too fast.

But for now my pleasure, and my distraction, is *andante*. *Andante moderato*. Or *andante sostenuto*, that is, sustained. And my vehicle is *A Treasury of Grand Opera*. In this time of social isolation, in a time of confinement and consideration, and of fear, I take my pleasures where I can, and join others in looking around ourselves for who we are.

These days, glancing behind reveals a landscape in which many things suddenly seem as antique as those dusty shops with outworn objects. A great crowd of people is in movement, and I can hear some of them, distantly and perhaps approaching, crying *morte,* death! And some of them are walking steadily and strongly, among them dragoons, gypsies, smugglers, cigarette girls, officials and urchins, and everyone I know and love. I can hear them singing *corragio,* courage. Courage!

(2020)

Meeting Harriet

Those who read history are blessed or cursed with double vision. We see the present as normal people do, but we also glimpse, in ghostly overlay, the shades of the sepia past. Unscarred land, settlements and villages, canoes and bateaux and paddleboats and levees drift and drape over the present landscape. Sometimes we can see, and sometimes hear, people moving over the land, exploring, setting cornerstones, living out their lives in the populated past.

And sometimes, when we keep our eyes open to the doubling and stop to read the small signage of the world, those distant dead, animated by our notice, can reach out from the past into the present, tap us on the shoulder, and lead us back into their lives.

That's what Harriet did for me.

I nearly ruined my legs and knees and lungs one day last summer climbing a bluff above a river town in Iowa. I'd chosen the area for its serenity, but for me as for most people, the ideal of quiet is nearly always tempered by the need to be available. So, after arriving and settling in and admiring the wide curve of the Mississippi, with the town of Lansing on its edge, the bluffs towering above and the eagles (or perhaps they were turkey vultures) higher still, I dutifully flipped open my cell phone only to discover an unanticipated kinship with my historical predecessors. I was, as they had been, completely out of touch with anyone outside my immediate field of vision. No signal, and no backup. The shell of a pay phone still stood down by the ball field, but only ragged wires remained.

There's one sure place to go for good information in a small town, and that is the public library, where the sympathetic ladies had a single suggestion. Go to the top of Mount Hosmer, to the city park, up near the turkey vultures, in order to . . . what? To be closer to the cell phone satellite? To establish line of sight with my home phone in distant Minnesota? Someone, at some time, they thought, had gotten a signal up there. I should try.

It was a warm afternoon, with a high, cloudless blue sky. I had a water bottle, was lightly dressed, and needed the exercise.

It took one hour and fifteen minutes of constant climbing to reach the top of Mount Hosmer on a closely curving paved road, pitched like a StairMaster. On my left, boulders and dense woods reaching toward the sky. On my right, an alpine slope to certain impalement on the town's steeples. The warm afternoon turned into a hot afternoon, or perhaps I was growing closer to the sun's corona. No one drove by; I would have dropped on my knees and begged for a lift. I couldn't call for help; my cell phone still wouldn't work. If I turned around, I was afraid I would just start rolling back down and that would be the end.

When the narrow road finally flattened and opened out into a wide park with tall trees and hummingbirds, I rested, panting, on a stone wall, looking down on the town and the distant roof of the public library. I saw two tiny figures come out the back door, tip their heads back, shade their eyes, and point upward in my direction. I waved.

I *could* see Minnesota, I thought. And a wide sweep of Wisconsin and the place where more rivers joined the labyrinthine Mississippi and its broad braid of wetlands and water and woods. A turkey vulture flew by, below me. The cell phone didn't work.

I walked through the park, which was deserted. A car appeared, and I resented its intrusion for a minute, but it drove right back down. There was a veterans' memorial and a playground. There were picnic benches. And there was a small blue metal sign, put up by the Iowa sesquicentennial commission a few years earlier, long enough ago for the bolts to rust a bit. I stopped to read it, and here is what the sign said, and this is how people who love history end up getting lost in their research.

> Mount Hosmer City Park was named after Harriet
> Hosmer, a noted sculptress, who won a foot race
> to the summit during a steamboat layover in 1851.

I stood there, sweating and still breathing hard, and read it again. A sculptress. Ran a foot race. During a steamboat layover in 1851.

In 1851, upper-class women were wearing six or perhaps eight heavy petticoats under dresses with long, dragging skirts and tight sleeves. Propriety called for an unnaturally narrow waist, bound by tightly laced corsets stiffened with whalebone or steel. Women of that period commonly relied on banisters to climb stairs; servants had to carry the lamp and the children. The sculptress had run a footrace?

In the next few months, I spent some time reading up on Harriet Hosmer. She was twenty-one in 1851, the daughter of a liberal Unitarian family in Watertown, Massachusetts. She was said to be athletic. Some sources said she'd been raised by her father as a boy, after the deaths from tuberculosis of her mother and a sibling.

Hosmer was midway through a highly adventurous steamboat journey, first from St. Louis to New Orleans and back, and then aboard a "floating palace" called *The Senator* going from St. Louis all the way upriver to St. Paul. She was traveling with a female companion and no chaperone, a highly unusual state of affairs. The trip was paid for by an indulgent and wealthy mentor, who later became the president of Washington University in St. Louis. The contemporary material referred to this journey as her travels "in the Western Wilderness."

The Senator had pulled in at Lansing to let off a passenger for Galena, Illinois, and to take on wood to feed its boilers. Miss Hosmer came out on deck to admire the scenery and then asked Captain Oren Smith if she would have time to climb to the top of the bluff. An unnamed gentleman offered to escort her. Smiling, she challenged him to a foot race.

The story was collected some ninety years later from a woman who claimed to have been a witness and must have been a child at the time.

> *They started up the bluff. She was soon far in advance of her escort. She went up toward an opening in the cliff, veered around the protruding rocks at the end of the cliff, then, striking the old Indian trail that followed the brow of the bluff, soon gained the summit. While her valiant squire was pantingly trying to catch up, Miss Hosmer stood waving her handkerchief at the stewardess who, standing on the guard of the boat, was frantically ringing the breakfast bell and shaking her turbaned head. Miss Hosmer met her companion on the way down.*

The defeated gentleman suggested to two local worthies breakfasting with the captain that the bluff be named after her, and Harriet Hosmer "graciously accepted," reported the witness. "She was very pleasing in manner and appearance, rather tall and slender. She appeared to have a remarkable personality." The witness recalled her child conversation with Miss Hosmer: "She talked to me about the wildflowers and the birds, and asked me many questions. She noticed some wild strawberries growing nearby."

After her journeys in the western wilderness, Miss Hosmer did become a noted sculptor, and rather a scandal. In that following year, she decamped from Boston to Rome, making sculptures and selling them and living an unfettered life. She became part of a circle of intellectuals and hobnobbed with literary figures such as Robert and Elizabeth Barrett Browning and Nathaniel Hawthorne. Her personality was no longer reported as "remarkable." Now it was called "abrupt." She was known for her eccentric, practical style, her man-tailored jackets, and her short hair.

And perhaps my favorite detail, she was reported to have been working on the invention of a perpetual motion machine before her death in 1908.

Since my long climb up Mount Hosmer, I have grown very fond of Harriet in the way a person can become fond of the historical dead. You're interested in the events of their lives. You seize on any surviving glimpse of personality. You make a timeline, just to be sure you notice the amount of time they spent studying in Europe and the various ages they were when they touched the public record or made a certain splash somewhere. You read up on steamboats and artists and women of the period. You think about the sources of artistic inspiration and how they surface in a body of work. In wondering about how one climbs a bluff in a whalebone corset, you read about clothing of the period and about the beginnings of women's dress reform. You note that in June 1851 an East Coast ladies' magazine printed a fashion plate of a new kind of ladies garment, quite revolutionary. Bloomers were a variation on Turkish pantaloons, covered by a skirt to the knees with a loose tunic above. The operative word here is *pantaloon*. They were *pants*.

People who love history are always reassembling the world from disparate details. With no one to contradict you, you are free to imagine that athletic Harriet, the young, female artist from a prosperous liberal family, raised to be opinionated, saw the plate in *Godey's Lady's Magazine* and had her seamstress go to work.

You fill in the blanks, you allow the overlay, until one dreamy day at your desk, you see the steamboat, its fires banked, laid up at the levee in wild Iowa. Third-class passengers are trudging back and forth carrying wood to the boilers. The captain is breakfasting on the top deck with businessmen who are laying out a town. Playing on the bank is a small girl with an observant eye and a good memory. A young woman with a long and lively life ahead of her steps out of her cabin into the sun and shades her eyes to look up at the high bluff and what might be an eagle. There is banter between her and a gentleman, and a challenge. She retires briefly to her cabin and appears again, in bloomers. Sensation! And up the bluff she goes.

I was back in Lansing this year, thinking about Harriet and her history. I stopped at the library and bought some books from the sale table. I ran into a fellow who told me that he'd once had to call out the volunteer fire department to rescue two people who'd tried to descend the Mount Hosmer bluff without using the road.

I drove to the bluff top and stayed a long time, thinking about Harriet and her footrace and watching the Mississippi curl north and south to the horizon. I'd found one of her sculptures at the Art Institute of Chicago and two more at the American Art Museum at the Smithsonian in Washington, DC, and I had stood a long while in those places, too, trying to look through the marble to see the ghost of her hands and chisel.

In Chicago, her sculpture in serene white marble is a bust of Zenobia, Queen of Palmyra, a warrior queen who led a famous revolt against the Roman Empire. Nathaniel Hawthorne, I read, had written a novel featuring an exotic character named Zenobia. His novel was published just a few years earlier than the sculpture was created. The sculpture is inscribed on the back *fecit Romae*, meaning "made in Rome," where the young sculptor was acquainted with Hawthorne.

At the Smithsonian, two Hosmers, similar in size and spirit, flank a hallway. One of them is a likeness of the sprite Puck, round and naughty, seated on a broad mushroom, with what might be oak leaves scattered below. Hosmer carved it in 1856, I saw, five years after racing to the summit and then, triumphant, questioning a little girl about the local flowers and birds. Puck's hallway companion is a

Will-o'-the-Wisp of the same period. Near his plump toes, a turtle peers out from some aquatic vegetation. I like to think that the mushrooms, the layered leaves, and perhaps the turtle entered the mind of the young sculptor on the banks of the Mississippi River in Lansing, Iowa, on the day she ran the footrace in her scandalous bloomers.

(2018)

The Broncho Buster

I have a theory that a person who travels a great deal, like myself, who is away from home and home base a good deal of the time, has to develop protective habits, ongoing interests that provide a certain sense of continuity, even when any given month may find you in Tucson or Chicago or the Upper Midwest or, say, Denver. These interests should have several common characteristics—they should have variety within a theme, they should be rooted in whatever locale you are in, they should give you an excuse to talk to interesting people along the way. They should, above all, be portable. (Isn't there a television correspondent who does paintings of hotel lamps?)

My protective coloration of late has led me into a rather obscure, or at least out-of-fashion, branch of the fine arts. I'm getting interested in public statuary, those great bronze or marble monoliths that decorate parks and plazas and public buildings all across the country. You know. You've seen them. The big things featured on postcards with a building in the background? They seem to have been there forever, ignored in a way because of their very permanence. You ignore them, your parents ignored them, your grandparents may have ignored them, too. Only the pigeons pay close attention, and they are notoriously indiscriminate in choice of company.

There is some beautiful public sculpture in Denver. I like to think that I would have stood and applauded at the unveiling, for example, of *The Broncho Buster*, the huge bucking horse with masterful cowboy that stands in the Civic Center Park downtown. The way all that bronze is poised midair over two firmly planted forelegs, the rider waving his arm for balance and, we suspect, for a little flair besides. *The Broncho Buster* was unveiled in 1918, and it is a direct and immediate throwback to the time when a bucking horse and cowboy could frequently be seen on the streets and old west Denver was largely corrals and longhorns. The statue was modeled from life, with the sculptor, Alexander Phimister Proctor, carefully selecting both horse and rider. The cowboy is a fellow named Red, six foot three and from Pendleton, Oregon. In his autobiography, Proctor says, "If anyone gave him five dollars and a drink of whiskey, [Red] would ride one of the buffaloes. The Cayuse [the horse, gentle readers] was a wall-eyed brute, a direct offspring of the devil." Proctor was a kind of participatory sculptor, an "animalier" as the French called it, who worked with animals, often large ones, from life for his sculptures. He was once sketching intently close to the bars of a panther's cage and turned his back to get better light on the drawing. "Suddenly," he says, "I felt needle-sharp points in my shoulder. Leaping away from the cage, I turned to see the big male cat's foreleg—at least six feet long, it looked to be—stretched through the cage, my blood dripping from his claws. Then and there I learned an important lesson for an artist: never turn your back on a wild four-legged model!"

Proctor was, in fact, not much of a one for turning his back on anything. He was born in Ontario in 1862, and traveled from his country into this country by covered wagon. He grew up in Denver with two ambitions: to succeed as an artist and to become a great hunter. As a boy, the two were not always in concert—he didn't like his first art lessons because they interfered with baseball and rabbit hunting. The Proctor family spent summers in Grand Lake, traveling there in the covered wagon and living a rough outdoor life that delighted the boy. When he was sixteen, Proctor killed an elk and his first grizzly in a single day of hunting. The adult Proctor believed that an artist's work must reflect the life that he lives, and all his life he would return again and again to the West, hunting, fishing, trapping, living among the cowboys and Native Americans and using many of them as models. Eventually, he would bring his wife and all seven children along on those expeditions.

He studied, of course, in Paris and New York, and undertook many famous commissions, including sculpting the wonderful animals and décor for the Elephant House, the Lion House, and the Primate House at the Bronx Zoo. The mounted Native American figure, called *On the War Trail*, that stands opposite *The Broncho Buster* here in Denver is also a Proctor. Together, they are heroic in concept, let alone in execution—casting and erecting a statue that size. Remember that Proctor modeled that horse and cowboy Red from life. Here is his description of a day's work on that "Cayuse," the one you hardly glance at while fighting the traffic on Colfax:

> One day when Red brought him into the studio to pose, he nearly kicked my hat off my head with his left hind foot without seeming to move a muscle. Then began a scene that can be imagined better than described. The studio was only fourteen by sixteen, just large enough for a horse and two men if everyone was quiet. With a kicking and bucking horse, there was only room for the horse and one man, and that wasn't me. I had sometimes had

trouble in close quarters with wild animals but had always managed to save myself and my model. That time all I wanted to save was my hide. Stovepipe, splinters, boxes, table, and high profanity flew around for a time until Red finally got the beast settled down.

That was Pendleton, Oregon, 1915.

Red, incidentally, was later convicted of horse stealing.

I'm a visitor to Denver of the frequent variety, one who comes here to work and play fairly continuously. I don't get to do many real touristy things in Colorado. I've made the obligatory trip to Evergreen and a drive to Central City, but by and large, it's the city of Denver that I see when I'm here. Here are a few small thoughts in praise of the part of Denver I spend most of my time in: northwest Denver, an area of town I understand few visitors see, unless it's while driving through on their way to Elitch Gardens. But I stay there with friends while I'm in town, and I find it, in many ways, remarkable.

First there's a fact so simple that native Denverites, if there are any, will find it laughable. You see, if you just go west from there, you'll get to the mountains. I first discovered this on Forty-Fourth Avenue, when I took a wrong turn pulling out of a supermarket parking lot and looked up to see the Rockies look back at me, apparently from the end of the road. This does not happen in Chicago or Minneapolis, and it seemed miraculous to me that you could just drive along a normal residential street and, if you kept going, eventually go quite decidedly uphill. Even now, as a more seasoned visitor, having tried I-70 to the mountains or the Sixth Avenue Freeway to the mountains, I still like to forget the city map, choose some east/west street or avenue, and just turn left. Forty-Fourth, for example, takes you by Carramone's Fruit Market and the Wheatridge Farm Dairy and eventually right by the Colorado Railroad Museum. For someone who isn't trying to make it halfway across the range in one day and who likes to see what there is to see, it's better than the freeway.

And you go through some wonderful neighborhoods. Street after street has tall trees shading small brick houses with small brick porches, sprinklers rhythmically covering those tiny lawns, each backyard with its dog-in-residence, obligatory, belligerent. And, at almost every house, what is for this visitor the signature of the neighborhood and the city—the roses. We don't have roses like that where I come from. Maybe it's too cold or too wet or people just don't care for them, but I have never seen such cascades of color as seem to hang from every little brick porch in north Denver. When the city cools off at night and the sprinklers get down to serious business, the stroller can walk for blocks, admiring those little moist lawns and the luxurious flowers. If you're bold enough to walk the alleys, you can sometimes glimpse small, perfect gardens of vegetables and flowers. I'm sure there are other beautiful gardens in Denver, and larger specimens. But one of my best pastimes in this city is a walk or drive to admire the neighborhood roses, and maybe a lift of the eye to admire the neighborhood mountains, just at the end of the road.

(1981)

35

Inside the Old Guthrie Theater

One of the ongoing themes at Guthrie dinner parties is that of the young person whose life was changed by the big theater. It happened to me in 1973. I was green, but not so green as not to have already been through my own theater disaster, as it seems nearly all young theater enthusiasts must. At Indiana University, some graduate students—how much older they seemed!—announced plans to start their own theater. Would I come and be their first stage manager? I could "go Equity," whatever that was. On the day after graduation, I moved to Indianapolis. It turned out there wasn't any stage managing to be done over the summer. The theater had to be founded first, and by the time the fall opening came around, I was shaking hands at cocktail parties and writing promotional copy. The theater hired a more experienced stage manager, then a promotions person who actually knew something about promoting, and in January, I was "let go."

The technical director kindly suggested the Guthrie to me, and me to the Guthrie. I had an idea the theater was in Milwaukee. I packed my car with everything I owned and started driving north.

I was hired as the most junior assistant in group sales, although I didn't really know any groups. I worked on a regional wall map; we pushed a pin into every city from which groups of senior citizens traveled to the theater. I learned to lurk in the dark at the back of the house during rehearsals, watching the stage managers operate and listening to Michael Langham's British accent. So exotic. I leaned against the wall at staff parties. It was not a great season. In the fall, the budget went south, and I was called into the office of the redoubtable managing director. My barely-above-penury position was cut, and I was again let go.

I lived the customary wandering theater life for seven years, working here, working there, like so many others. I came back to the Guthrie in 1980 as stage manager for a small production, rapidly followed by big ones, and stayed nearly ten years making plays with Liviu Ciulei, with Lucian Pintilie, Peter Sellars, Garland Wright, and many more. I was a stage manager, then production stage manager, and eventually production manager, the boss job for all the producing departments of the theater. That work formed my personal aesthetic and taught me everything I know about standards. I hardly ever came out of the back stage on Vineland Place, even to get married and have my first child, who came to work with me at age three weeks. With my second, I realized I could do either the work or the parenting at that pace. I left the staff but kept the contact, writing regularly for the theater, seeing most shows, and over time gaining the longer view that daily production work absolutely eliminates.

I lunched regularly with Sheila Livingston, my former fellow traveler in senior citizen sales, who over time held nearly every position on the Guthrie staff. She knew almost everyone, and I knew the rest of them. We ate, we laughed, we repeated stories we'd seen or heard. Eventually we realized that the stories we told were largely unknown and that, however brief, acerbic, or even scatological, they were the truth about the Guthrie and the people who make it up. I started to write them down.

It is hard to decide on my favorite Guthrie story. It might be the night during the run of *Who's Afraid of Virginia Woolf?* when Patrick Stewart was on stage. Stewart has what you might call a strong following based on his years on television as a *Star Trek* captain; the theater invested in a new security system before his arrival in Minneapolis. As the story goes, one evening the doorbell rang at the stage door, and the night man pushed a button to activate the camera. On the little screen was a Klingon warrior in full regalia, demanding to see "Captain Picard." In the Klingon language. Through an interpreter (presumably Minnesotan, or at least earthling). There's another version of this story, in which the Klingon and interpreter come to the box office to buy tickets.

Or a wedding I attended on stage in 1988, on an off night from *Richard III*. The stage crew chief and his bride rose from the trap room below the stage aboard a gigantic Shakespearean throne, under ominous stage light with show music filling the house, with maybe seventy-five Guthrie folk and family sitting right down front.

I remember an enormous gospel choir standing up from the mass of onstage risers during the first preview of *The Gospel at Colonus*, following conductor J. D. Steele, swaying left, swaying right, opening their mouths to sing, and leaving the stunned audience with their hair standing on end from the power of the music.

There is a story told in the box office about a woman who was a Guthrie subscriber with her entire family for years. When she died, her family kept the seat and filled it with a dozen red roses for the rest of the season.

In a long and hilarious conversation with some impossibly inventive scene shop artisans, I was told a mischievous story about placing some leftover scrap steel—they always had plenty around—in the old upstairs lobby between the Guthrie and the rather formal Walker Art Center on Vineland Place, and fabricating a perfect Walker-looking modern-art-identifying plaque for it. It stood there in splendor for several weeks before the hoax was discovered.

I've heard a report from a visitor to the London apartment of the then elderly Tanya Moiseiwitsch, the astonishing and seminal designer who, with Tyrone Guthrie, designed the thrust stage in 1963. Among the memorabilia of her lifetime in the theater: a Minnesota Twins cap, sitting atop a bottle of scotch.

As the theater's production manager, I was often stunned by the detailed perfection the shops created. For a beautifully set period dinner table for *The House of Bernarda Alba* in 1987, the prop master researched exactly how dinner tables were set in rural Spain in 1900, fabricated what was needed, and provided the actors with an exquisitely complete, correct, and right world in which to play a crucial scene. There isn't even a photograph of that; I looked.

My favorite memory, though, probably is the sunny fall afternoon in 2003 when ground was broken for the new theater complex by the Mississippi River. The young actors from the theater's partnership program with the University of Minnesota, working for their bachelors of fine arts under the wing of the Guthrie, stood on risers singing their hearts out from Stephen Sondheim's *Merrily We Roll Along*. Each one was greatly talented. Each one was thinking inside, "Look at *me*! Look at *me*!"

"Feel the flow," they sang.

> *Hear what's happening:*
> *We're what's happening.*
> *Don't you know?*
> *We're the movers and we're the shapers.*
> *We're the names in tomorrow's papers.*
> *It's our time, breathe it in:*
> *Worlds to change and worlds to win.*
> *Our turn coming through.*
> *Me and you, pal,*
> *Me and you!*

Among the singers was Santino Fontana; two years later, he was cast to play Hamlet in the closing production at the old Guthrie on Vineland Place. It was his time.

Also in 2003, the actor Hume Cronyn, then nearing age ninety-two, returned to the Guthrie, where he'd first captivated audiences in *The Miser* in 1963. Seated on stage, Cronyn regaled the audience with tales both touching and ribald—and then delivered a speech from *Henry VI, Part 3*. All frailty fell away. He rose, crossed down left (with the lights dimming and following him), and held the audience spellbound with just words and actor power.

Cronyn had once written a letter to the acting company in which he said, "We are members of a preposterous and sentimental profession." Well, yes.

There is a convention in the theater called the "fourth wall," an invisible barrier that separates the players from the audience. On occasion, someone crashes through. Actor Peter Michael Goetz has been telling this story since a late Wednesday afternoon in June 1975, just after this very eventful matinee.

"I was playing in *Arsenic and Old Lace* in a scene with Barbara Bryne, somewhere in the first act. Two very old ladies had gotten away from the ushers. They made their first entrance into the theater at the top of what we called the Alpine Slope, the long aisle, and they came down, well, forever. One had a cane. *Boompity-boomp.* They were kind of talking and looking for their seats and they came all the way down to the gutter, near the stage. Then they crossed, and walked up the next aisle. From on stage, we'd see the door to the lobby open and close and we'd think, well, they're gone. Then at the top of the next aisle, the door would open and *boompity-boomp.* Down to the gutter, and around, and then back up; the door would close. It took about a half hour. Finally, they came right down and I was opening the window seat to discover the body and one woman came right up on the stage and said to me 'Can you help us find our seats?!' Barbara was laughing so hard that she left me on stage. I tried to say, 'We'll see what we can do.' We had to stop the play. It was incredible, incredible."

Barbara Bryne remembers another mishap in Act III of the very same performance:

"Then, later in the same matinee, well! As Abby Brewster, I wore a fob watch on the top right-hand side of my dress.

42

They have a little chain on them. Peter at one point asked me the time. "What time is it, Auntie?" I pulled out the watch on its chain and somehow, I don't know how, the chain of the fob watch caught on a drop earring I was wearing, and my head jerked to one side. Peter asked me for the time three times; every time he asked me, my head shot to one side. This sight was too much for Peter, who ran up the staircase on the set and left me alone on stage. The next few minutes were very tricky trying to control the giggles."

There is something about first rehearsal days that contain the entire heart of the theater.

There is a room deep in the lower regions of the Guthrie Theater that most people never see. It sits at the end of a long hallway at the bottom of a stairwell. It is not slick or shiny; it has nothing comfortable about it. But it is a magic space to the people who work in it, a private, intense space that has the capacity to entirely shut out the world outside. Rehearsal Room 1 is where the art is prepared for the audience.

The room is high and bare and a bit shabby. It's been painted a few times, most recently two years ago between seasons. It had been a kind of muddy yellow; the new color was chosen by the simple system of painting large sample swatches on the wall and polling the room's regular occupants for their opinions. Then it was painted a kind of muddy white.

The paint job didn't do much for the room's overall sparseness—maybe brightened it a little, maybe freshened it a little. But now, two years later, it is still high and bare and shabby. One wall of the room, at the tallest end, is covered with old velvet curtains. The curtains look like they might have been buried somewhere damp for a long time. There's a reason for this. In addition to normal wear and tear, the curtains fell victim to an idea in the early eighties that the room was often too dry for the hard vocal work of daily rehearsals, and the way to make it better was to spray down the curtains with a hose. As they dried, so the theory went, the humidity in the room would improve. It didn't work very well: the hose was heavy and the water puddled and the floor warped. And the curtains developed giant, permanent water stains.

Behind the curtains are dance mirrors, and most of the room is covered with a shop-made Masonite floor, slightly elevated from the tile and much scarred with tape and furniture marks. Both were added when the theater started doing musicals. Dancers need mirrors to perfect their moves and sprung floors to protect their legs and feet.

There's a skylight in Rehearsal Room 1. On bright sunny days, the room is decorated with a large, square shaft of light that travels across the playing area as the afternoon goes on. Actors move through it as they go about rehearsal; sometimes a climactic moment in the play happens to take place in a blaze of brilliant light.

Between rehearsal periods, the room is used for many different purposes. The actors in the playing show use it for their warm-ups. Since the playing show is a musical this year, the room's height is filled eight times a week with voices that begin with vowels and scales and end in full-throated song. The crew for the playing show comes in to play basketball in it. Once the stage is set and all is in order, the stagehands come down and strip off their shirts and work out against a backboard that the shop suspended from the lighting bridge. There are classes in it, and auditions: earnest young actors perform Laura's speech from *The Glass Menagerie* after walking a little timidly down the hallway past the shops. And the shops use it for overflow space, laying out a huge china silk drop for cutting and sewing, or planning the intricacies of a plank floor.

For the last few weeks, the shops have had a bigger project in this room. The shows in preparation for the new season are a cycle of three Shakespeare histories: *Richard II*, *Henry IV, Parts 1 and 2*, and *Henry V*. Codirectors Garland Wright and Charles Newell and scenic designer Douglas Stein have settled that the histories will be performed on the old stage shape, the original asymmetry that Tanya Moiseiwitsch and Dr. Guthrie himself first chose in 1963. So the theater has built a rehearsal set to that exact shape. Its height, three surrounding steps, and its odd angles, dominate the room.

On this day, March 13, 1990, RR1 returns to its primary use. All other work becomes entirely secondary. On this day, rehearsals begin for the new season. The actors are coming. With them, they bring all possibility, all audacity, and sheer nerve.

The stage management staff has been at work all morning. At each place at the circle of tables, high up on the mock stage, is a pencil and a little pad of paper. There are twenty-eight stacks of three bound scripts, mute testimony to the sheer size of the coming project. Off to the side is a table for the stage manager's setups, prompt scripts and yellow pads, telephone and a bowl of hard candy. At stage manager Jill Rendall's chair is a vase of daffodils. In the brown and muddy white and gray of the room, they are violently yellow. At one edge, someone has set an effigy prop from last season's production of *The Screens*, a Styrofoam soldier with bared teeth that towers over the tables. On the director's table, where Wright will settle, the prop crown from 1983's satiric *Merry Wives of Windsor* is sitting. The crown is ridiculously velvet and topped with a stuffed corgi; it will disappear before rehearsal begins.

On one scarred wall of RR1, dramaturg Michael Lupu is putting up research materials, a large spreadsheet of historical information about each principal character in the plays, and a long, handmade banner reading "All things are ready if our minds be so." The quote is from *Henry V*. "Jill," he calls out in his Romanian-accented English. "The daffodils, they should have been fleur de lis. But no! That is my job, that whatever we do, I explain how right it is. My job is to explain how daffodils *are* fleur de lis!" Laughter.

Good humor abounds on first rehearsal days. The stage managers joke that they will deliver the *Henry V* St. Crispin's Day speech weeks from now on the first day of dress rehearsals, presumably the part about "He that outlives this day, and comes safe home." There is an air of anticipatory excitement in the room.

A little after eleven, the crowd starts to come in. Many of the theater staff arrive to meet and welcome the company back from their break. Veteran company member John Lewin gasps a little when he sees the shape of the rehearsal stage and exclaims, in broad British, "It's Tanya's stage!" Lewin has spent eleven seasons here, of the theater's twenty-six. When he climbs up the steps, he glances around in a satisfied manner—he knows this shape. "I've bruised my shin on it so many times!"

The company chatters. *You've lost weight, you've gained weight, you've had a baby! I'm getting a nosebleed up here*, from the height of the mock stage. Stephen Pelinski has been cast as fiery Hotspur. Someone says, "Oh, you're playing the wild man," and Pelinski replies, grinning, "No, he's just misunderstood, man, just misunderstood."

There is an announcement that new script pages can be found on top of each tall stack of scripts. Groans ensue: "Additions rather than subtractions?" Actor bags, the industry equivalent of gym bags, appear by all the chairs, stuffed with clothes and shoes and reference texts. Sandwiches, bottles of water, cups of coffee, and gooey donuts from the big box in the corner appear on the tables. Actor Steve Yoakam takes one look at the setup and marches down from the stage. He is going for a more comfortable chair. With three plays to read, it will be a long haul.

There is some business to be done. Forms to fill out, introductions to be made, a few words about cuts and vocal work and the evolving design. Finally, Garland Wright smiles a little and says, "Let's read *Richard II*." There is much clearing of throats, much rustling and bustling. Then the room falls absolutely quiet. The stage manager looks inquiringly at Wright and then nods, smiling, to Charles Janasz, who, as King Richard, has the opening lines in the first of the three plays. Charlie smiles and takes a breath. The shaft of sunlight, very bright, is about center in the room. And the work begins.

(1990, 2006, 2020)

Verse II

LOOKING BACK

How the Bubble Tree Came to Me

Christmas casts its rosy glow over the past for many people, and for me. And if the season is sentimental and softening, if it dims the vision and favors fond detail over narrative, it is also true that the snow lay deep in December in the town I grew up in, and houses were gilded with lights, and on Christmas Eve, in our matching pajamas, we were driven in the big car through the neighborhoods we knew, and places we'd never been, kneeling up to look out the back seat windows, scrubbing away the fog of our own breath with our flannelled elbows. It was all primary colors and Santas in sleighs and Nativity sets in a real shed made of plywood and filled with hay. Through picture windows, the trees were twinkling, some green like our own, but others puffily frosted in white and a few entirely silver and metallic and *turning*. I always wondered why the extension cords didn't wind up and tip them over.

Continuous carols played on the radio. The snow fell. My father drove. Christmas, I'm sure, cast its brief radiance over his past, too. Perhaps my parents saw the season in a kind of double vision, as I do now. You see what is before you and also what is no longer there, and everything through the soft tunnel of memory. My mother, for example, remembers midnight Mass, and that would have meant the seeing-the-lights trip on another night, or at least no pajamas. No matter, no matter.

We had no picture window at the house on Braeburn, but we did have a tremendous fireplace in the living room, and its outside face was trimmed, I think, by a wreath. Or am I making that up? I do remember the moment of pulling back into our own driveway after seeing the town, and some dim contentment about the look of our own house. It was beautiful, with large windows and an oaken front door framed in glass. There was a coach light, I think, and it would have been trimmed for the season in greenery and light. We ran up the sidewalk in our pajamas and our boots, past the three cutout caroling choirboys, and tumbled in under the tree for cocoa in the special Santa cups and one package to open from the wrapped piles, carefully separated into three, and later four, stacks. My small sister, burdened early with a sense of aesthetics or perhaps it was a sense of justice, would have spent hours arranging the piles so that they appeared exactly the same size, with the same, well, curb appeal.

Wrapped packages, cups of cocoa, candles lit on the mantel above the fire. Decades later, and in the absence of corroboration, it could be a single moment made iconic by time or many Christmases strung together, the way old home movies can be joined into a single reel. I cannot see a way to be sure.

I do remember hiding under the tree, which stood in a corner of the high-ceilinged living room. Our trees were not bushy or thick, but they were very tall, with long, spare branches (my mother said the balsams showed off the ornaments better), and the metal stand stood them off the floor some little distance. There was room for a small girl to wriggle under and lie on her back safe in the corner, where no one could see. Sometimes I took a little pillow to soften the unyielding floor. Looking up was gazing into a complex star system of branches and shiny ornaments and cords and light. The end of every branch was heavy with tinsel, each shimmery strand separately hung for maximum sparkle. They moved a little with my breath, and in the air of the room as people moved by, speaking, unaware of me.

We had two houses for Christmas mornings when I was a child. Our big grand house was across the street from the small one where my mother had grown up, and where her parents and sister still lived. In that house was another tree and another pile of presents and another set of decorations and cards and candles. After we had happily torn our stacks to pieces at home, we would catch a fever to be gone and, pulling on our jackets and boots over those ubiquitous Christmas pajamas, we would tear down the sidewalk and across the street and across the big yard toward our grandparents' house, fleeing from one house, descending on the other, where I would see Grandma Bea looking out the front window and smiling as we came. They would have already had their breakfast, and the arrival of the grandchildren was the Main Event, as we well knew. We'd open our presents, and we'd sit for cinnamon toast at the big round dining room table that practically filled the room, and I'd look out the bay window at cardinals coming to the feeder in the snow. And Beatty would smile at me, reach down the side of the tea cart, and turn on the Bubble Tree.

Sometime in the holiday season of 1952 or 1953, I think, my aunt Jane was hurrying through the main floor of the State Street Marshall Field's in Chicago. In those days, and for decades, the main floor of Field's was a city block square, three stories tall, and studded with enormous columns that probably actually did hold up the nine retail floors above. Around the giant pillars and their overscale capitals were fabulous holiday decorations, on a scale to suit the setting. Gigantic round-bellied snowmen leaning outward, and shiny Christmas balls two feet in diameter, hung with wide red ribbons and enormous bows. On the marble floor were aisle after aisle of shining cases with the best of goods arrayed for Chicagoans, and well-dressed decorous saleswomen saying, "May I wrap this for you, madam?" as people bustled by. Oh, it was a palace.

My aunt was thirty-five then, a petite and energetic woman, properly gloved and hatted and wrapped in a winter coat. She carried a pocketbook and, for some reason, on this particular December afternoon, she also carried little me, her namesake, called Peggy Jane. I suppose I was properly gloved and hatted, too, and decorous, looking up at the decorations with that small-child serenity, hearing the city chatter around us, headed for the train to go home. I was a biddable child, I think, and it must have been quite a shock to Jane when I leaned and reached for the Bubble Tree.

"You nearly tipped me over! And when I stopped, you were looking and looking at something on one of the counters, all lit up. It was a bubble tree, all lit and bright, and you wanted it so much. You fell in love with it, I think."

I think I did, and perhaps it was the first fall after milk and mother. The impulse to lean toward something has lasted; I have, ever since, had the capacity to be suddenly caught and held. I have fallen in love regularly and permanently, with the shape of horses, with flat golden afternoon light, with the charged alchemy of the rehearsal room, with the faces of my children, with the intersection of words. And on that day it was a little tabletop tree, electrified, and, on the tip of every branch, lights bicolored and glass-tubed, each one bubbling hard toward its tip. It was marked $16.47.

Now, let me be clear. My aunt was a frugal woman, trained in a hard school of frugality. My grandparents' home, and hers, was modest and mostly hand-built. Everything was used and reused, and Jane was well established in a lifelong scrounging habit—no pile of furniture marked "free" ever went unexamined. The clothes she was wearing that day in Field's are probably still hanging in her dark closet. The war had brought the country out of the Great Depression, and it was early in the prosperous fifties, but that family had embraced skimping and saving as their way of life.

But we were having a Special Day, and, she says, my eyes were large and round and filled with light. Janie stopped at the counter and bought the bubble tree in its big box and lugged it home on the train, and later that night, her mother set it on the tea cart against the bay window and we all watched it light up and begin to bubble, its image doubled by the storm window and magnified by the many little curving panes. Outside, the snow fell, I suppose, and it was cold. Inside, I sat with my grandparents and my namesake aunt and watched the bright bubbling begin.

I have it now. It came to me sometime in the 1980s, when I was living in a settled house at last and had settled work, and it must have looked as if my young wandering days were over. Unbelievably, I brought it home on an airplane—was I out of my mind?—in its own original storage box, still marked Marshall Field and Company, on

55

which I scribbled in large red letters "FRAGILE" and "UP" with many demonstrating arrows. It has been the signature event of my own holidays for thirty-five years, and the start of a bubble forest of sorts, as my husband and I would run across other trees in shabby antique stores. One season, after realizing, with a start, that there would come a day when all the bulbs we had would have burned out and then the bubble tree era would end, we started a deliberate search for the old small-based bulbs. Now, I shudder to report, we have several hundred bulbs, and most of them work. We save the others just in case. The bubble tree era extends into our children's futures, and perhaps their children's.

We don't have a bay window in this house, but at holiday time, we put all the leaves in our dining room table and run it right up against the windows, crowding the trees up against the pane. An extended period, sometimes a week or two, of delicate adjustment follows, as the bulbs are tested and settled and the old cloth-covered electrical cords run to the outlets. We moan a little, seeing that some "needles" are dropping, never to return. We chase off the damned cat, who as a kitten thought the needles strangely delicious. And then one Minnesota night, perhaps with icicles outside the window, and some years with heavy frost on the pane, when we're all home together, we light the bubble trees one by one against the dark. We struggle with the ancient frayed cords and the sockets where connection is prevented by bits of viscose. We agree that the oldest bulbs work best and that the family tree is the most important. We test, and test again, to find which is the failed bulb that prevents a tree from lighting, and eventually we settle for what we can. The bubble forest has upward movement and color, doubled by reflection and multiplied by memory. In the dark outside the pane, behind my own face and in what would be the stars over the trees, I think I glimpse my mother, my brothers and sister, and my grandmother, eyes cast down as she moves toward the kitchen.

Christmas!

(2010)

Letters from a Country Gone

My grandfather's letters were all written to other people and came to me a few years ago still contained in a battered manila envelope, postmark faded to a dim pink barely readable as sometime in July 1978. The envelope was addressed to my aunt Jane, who, by that time, was alone in the house on Lake Michigan. Frank had died the year before, in May, giving up the ghost in the night in the narrow bed by the lakeside window, always cracked to admit the sound of the waves. I sleep in that bed sometimes now when I'm visiting; there is a mirror by its foot with a crucifix above it, festooned with long, dry fronds from many past Palm Sundays. Sometimes I wonder if my grandfather could see himself in it as he lay there.

There are phrases that occur and recur in the letters, and capitalizing that represents emphasis; in the live telling, that would have been a rap on the table, a laugh followed by a coughing spell. "In my day . . ." he says repeatedly, and "in that country . . ." and it is not merely an old man's locution. He means that "that country" no longer exists and that that day was his, and the modern one was not. I remember how he closed up the ramparts of his small family's life against the sixties and its agitations, and how he watched the grandchildren grow into lanky loungers in ragged jeans who drove too fast up the winding driveway to the lake house. We were not, I think, interested in his stories, to my shame. He writes in one letter, about the four of us, "a pretty good group, but there are times when a good clean murder might be the simplest solution." Worth a chuckle when we were small and adoring, and maybe not so much when we were not.

And he was much given to the word "etc.," used as

shorthand to indicate everything his correspondents already knew about the lost geography he described. Now the correspondents are all gone, too, and "etc." means nothing at all.

The world of the letters, so alive in his memory and so affectionately described, is the world, I rather hope, that he traveled back to as his body failed. Fort Worth, Texas, around the year 1900.

I was raised in the country, on a place of 185,000 acres, a band of some 600 horses and at times as many as 20,000 cattle. Of course the values were very different than today, for at that time, you could buy all the land you could see for $1.25 an acre or lease it for 6 cents an acre a year.

We used to figure it required twenty acres of grass to support an animal, but in good years, with plenty of rain and good grass, we'd increase the run. When the grass was poor we'd have to reduce the run to maybe 8 or 10,000 head.

There were four boys and we had the usual array of horses, ponies, cattle, dogs, cats, guinea pigs, prairie dogs, chickens and most anything that was "pettable." At one time we had a cinnamon bear until it grew up and was too rough on our dogs; another time we had a pet antelope, but the game warden insisted on its release. It was said many times by friends, neighbors and the like that they could never understand how our mother lived to 76 years with the four of us. What one didn't think of, the other did.

We kids were always trying something like shoeing horses, repairing wind mills, erecting fence, building pens, etc etc. On the place we had a complete black smith shop, plumbing shop, machine shop, carpenter shop so were prepared to repair anything from a saddle to an engine. We kids did a big business loaning tools to the Mexican freighter teams (10 to 20 animals, horses or mules, to a team) for repairing a wagon or harness and in return they would bring us pets—prairie dogs, chipmunks, lizards, horned toads, birds, chickens and the like—until the place resembled a ZOO.

As kids, my brothers and I just lived for the annual events of rodeos and circuses. In my day the name rodeo had not been invented—it was known as a "contest" and in town was usually held in a ball park, but out in the country out on the open prairie. Out there it was not impossible for a horse or steer or bull to get scot free and take off for the "woods" with somebody's rope or saddle attached. Then, much commotion ensued, as in that country to lose any of your equipment because of wild or unruly stock was the height of disgrace.

In my time all camp gear, chuck wagon, etc were moved from pasture to pasture, or range, with mules and wagons plus camp cooks which might be black, or white, or Mexican, or Chinese, but ALWAYS MEN. The crew fed at a campfire and all slept on the ground. If a rainstorm came up there would be a mad rush to get beneath the chuck wagon as the only dry spot. One man spent his time finding and bringing in firewood. In the old days "frijole" beans were the main dish along with boiled salt pork and at supper, or in very cold weather COFFEE ROYALE (in a one gallon pot with one quart of whisky added). We went to town just two times a year, at Xmas and at election, and maybe a special trip for a circus. We were 95 miles from town, a 1 ½ to 2 day trip. We used to move our range horses at about 5–6 miles an hour. No horses were fed grain, everything was grass fed so were "soft" and used but one day a week. Every man had seven horses in a mount—six were his working horses and one his SUNDAY HORSE, which he only used to call on his girl or go to town by.

In time, the family moved into North Fort Worth, where they lived at 1700 Grand Avenue, before many streets were laid out. The boys watched the end of cattle drives from the roof of the house, as the stock was driven toward the yards. The town was rambunctious, and the letters are filled with character sketches.

Old Mr. Craig was guard on a chain gang and when we kids would visit the camp, he would invite us to eat the beans and biscuits. He was the one armed guard who always had the worst prisoners, the ones with two picks on their legs. Then there was Andy Mansker, a little bit of a fellow but rather fearless with that big gun. He used to invite me to hold and watch his horse and buggy while he served papers or made rounds. I was with him when he shot and killed a man at the GREY MULE SALOON in downtown Fort Worth.

The jail consisted of an iron cage about 8 x 8 x 7 feet in a wooden shack with no running water nor sanitary facilities. It was located about two blocks from the school so each day, we kids would have to go by to see who was locked up, and get him or her drinking water and maybe something to eat for the night. We used to hang around the City Hall where the Police were. The Police used horses and buggies for their hurry-up calls and would always take one of us along to "hold the horse" when he jumped out and caught the culprit, or most often shot him. I recall once the Worth Hotel clerk had been held up, so I was with the Police that were first there. The officer went into the hotel, and I tied the horse, not wanting to miss a single thing. The officer asked the clerk "what did the gun look like?" and the clerk quickly answered "it looked like a sewer pipe to me!" I was thoroughly bawled out for tying up the horse and then being in the way.

Of course, every kid had his horse. In summer we could get
odd jobs to earn a little money; during the school year it was
hard to earn. Every house had a cow or two and they could
eat a lot of hay penned up all the time, so we kids had a
"route." We'd take the cows out in the morning before school
and then bring them home after school. For that we charged
$1 per month per cow. We could handle about 25 or 30
cows but of course we always had to have a partner—more
for company than work. After the first week, the cows would
be waiting at the gate to get started in the morning and at
night they were anxious to get home for the milking and
some solid feed. They knew the way to and from the pasture
better than we kids, but we still had to go along to justify
our fee.

They were rascals, those boys, no doubt. Three close in age
and one a bit younger, and Frank the oldest. A trial to their
mother, who seems to have handled some of the most lively
situations with a buggy whip, and to their father, who was
the superintendent for Swift and Company at the Fort
Worth Stockyards. The photography of the time casts a
serious air on its subjects, but it is clear that John William
Condon was an imposing man. It is more difficult to tell at
this remove if he was proud of his rascal boys or not. As
old men themselves, the brothers referred to their father as
the Old Gent, or JW for John William. And they
remembered their own sobriquet, apparently in general use
in Fort Worth, around the yards and beyond. They were
called "those damned Condon kids."

Remember old Mrs. Collins? Frank wrote to his brother Tex in
1964. *I remember that picket fence being a block long but I suppose it*
was only 100 or so feet. Anyway, we kids would have a slat or flat
piece of wood and run alongside the fence dragging the stick along the

pickets. One kid was enough but when half a dozen did it, the old girl would be out there yelling like a Comanche—the noise was terrible! She was always going to have us killed if we didn't stop bothering her! And Tex wrote back laconically . . . *yes, yes, she <u>would</u> rave on, referring to our ancestry.*

Frank again: *Do you remember when we got the job of churning butter and separating milk at Striplings Dairy? Of course the churn and separator were hand driven and it was essential that they be operated at a consistent speed. The deal was that we were to get 5 cents for each batch, plus milk to drink. The first few times, the milk to drink was fine, but it wasn't long until we commenced to get ideas. The main one was to drink CREAM instead of the milk. I guess old Strip noticed a fall off in cream percentage; the job played out quite suddenly.*

One of my numerous summer jobs, at about age 13, was to bring horses from the Exchange Building tie racks, where all buyers, sellers, speculators, yard employees gathered while the buyers and sellers argued and traded. I took the horses to the blacksmith shop for shoeing and returned them when shod; horses always required new shoes periodically as hard roads were coming into vogue. This job was quite dull and there was a goat there that probably found time a little heavy on his hands too. He was a large Angora, just an old pet we played with at odd times. One of us conceived the idea that we should train Bill the goat, so we proceeded to train him to butt a feed bucket. We'd push it against his head and then back off a little; then when he came forward for some feed, we'd bang the bucket against his horns. It didn't take him too long to realize that feed buckets were both his friend and his enemy—his friend because they meant something to eat, and his enemy because he had to butt them in order to get the food. The net result was that all buckets were to be butted.

After this training, Bill was ready to attack any bucket. So we'd sit up in front of the shop and when some workman with a lunch bucket came along we'd simply point Bill in his direction. Before you'd know it the bucket would be sailing through the air, and sometimes the

*carrier, too, and we'd be busy capturing old Bill and giving apologies
and also preparing for the next attack.*

Bill later inherited a job as Judas goat at the slaughterhouse,
but he apparently still didn't escape the attentions of the
Condon boys.

*I recall the time we felt poor old Bill was too warm, and should be
clipped. After much wrestling with him and with hand clippers the job
was finally completed, but sometime during the night poor old Bill
departed this world. We suspected the cause was his embarrassment.*

And there was the story of the bear and the banty chicks,
which I remember hearing while turning the handle of an
old ice cream churn on Sunday afternoons. As I recall, a
good deal of chortling was involved in the telling.

*At about fifteen years of age, I worked a summer vacation on a ranch
at Ozona, Texas* [he identifies the ranch by its brand, "09"]
*and for three months I earned (or at least I was paid) $60. Coming
home I transferred trains at Brownwood Junction and had about a
two-hour layover. In roaming around, I found a middle-sized bear
chained in front of a restaurant who was quite gentle, and to whom I
was attracted. To make a long story short, I ended up as owner of the
bear, but minus 57 of my hard-earned dollars. When the train
arrived, the conductor refused to let me on with the bear. After much
imploring on my part, the conductor agreed that the bear and I could
ride in the baggage car if I purchased two tickets. That ate up all my
money and when we arrived at the home town, I had to send for a
horse and buggy to get the bear out home. Do you know how a half-
wild horse acts in the presence of a bear? At home I had to placate my
father as well as all the other horses in the lot, which was no easy job.*

*In time, the bear, horses and family became adjusted to one another
and my trading instinct came out. I started to rent the bear on a chain
to neighbor kids so they could play with him. Before long I had most of
the small change in the neighborhood and was reduced to letting some
kid play with the bear for whatever he wanted to trade. All kids had*

Banty chickens so before long I had quite a flock. That, however, didn't last too long. The Bantys ran with the regular chickens and my mother discovered the cause of the reduced-size eggs. As a result my project had to be abandoned and bear and Bantys disposed of.

But their best prank, the one Tex called *the premiere of all times*, was the night they soaped the streetcar tracks. The Northern Texas Traction streetcars had a hand brake, and for a while the brothers had a friendly relationship with Bagley the motorman, who used to let them turn the trolley at the terminus of the line and get a free ride for a block or two. That was before the event in question, involving the Condon boys, the hill on the streetcar line, and what must have been a considerable quantity of soap.

We soaped the tracks on the down hill side toward 20th Street, and when the car hit the soap, it just slid past every one who was waiting for a ride into town. It's a wonder that the car didn't fly the track. I can see Bagley right now frantically trying to make that old hand brake hold and the harder he pulled the tighter the brakes locked; the car just gained momentum all the time. I think it slid for ten or eleven blocks! Old man Bagley carried a hog leg six-shooter as big as the side of a house. He said that no one but a GODDAMN Condon kid would do a thing like that, and that he would shoot any of us on sight. When he finally got stopped, he tried to come back up the hill to catch us but he couldn't make it. He just kept sliding back. We were long gone, high tailing it for home to make up some sort of alibi.

I was back in Fort Worth a few years ago, Tex wrote back, *and walking to the Yards. On the way I passed a barber shop and thought "Well, I think I will get shaved here." The barber was working on me; he had put a hot towel on my face when a streetcar went by. I said "I remember well when this streetcar line was established." I told him about the incident of soaping the tracks and he grabbed the towel from*

66

my face and said "Are you one of those goddamn Condon kids?"

As the oldest, Frank had a wide variety of jobs from a young age, most of them around livestock and many of them associated with the "family business," Swift and Company.

I used to help out the stenos in the National Commission office, when they were getting out their Saturday market letter. They gave me a meal ticket for the restaurant at the Yards instead of money—I guess they could cover it up easier. It was supposed to be used up at one meal. I didn't need full meals, but I did want pie and ice cream. So I made a deal with the restaurant man to give me pie a la mode each day for a week and then turn in the $1.20 meal ticket. Some shenanigans. Not much money but PLENTY of pie a la mode.

When I was about 15 or 16, I gathered up about a dozen burros and drove them to Mineral Wells, Texas, which was quite a health resort, and sold them to a fellow who rented them out for folks to ride up the hills which the concessionaire called "mountains." I don't recall how much I made on the deal, but it financed a week's vacation for me at the Sangcura Wells resort.

Another experience [and here I imagine my grandfather pouring his signature fudge into a cake pan to cool as he talked] *was the time I shipped two cars of horses for Cook and Simmons, to Miller Bros 101 Ranch, the show folks, at Bliss, Oklahoma. Ed England was supposed to ship with them but couldn't be found at train time, so I was elected. It was my first trip, I guess, and I had no sleep during the ride—those railroad brakemen wouldn't give you the time of day when you were shipping. I arrived dead tired. At the ranch they were rehearsing the show for going on the road, and a few of the ranch hands were going to hunt a panther that had killed a colt the night before. Although invited to go along, I was too tired, so I went to their "dog house," the bunk house. I was sleeping good when I suddenly awoke with a start, and in the doorway stood this big*

Indian in his feathers, etc. Well, it was his dress rehearsal outfit, but all I could think of was that he was there to scalp me. I quick decided to go hunting the bobcat. I wanted no part of that Indian business, either domesticated or wild. My only thought was of the Indian raids that old Mr. Alderman used to tell about.

The dress rehearsal would have been for the 101 Ranch Wild West Show, which toured nationally starting in 1907 and boasted famous performers such as Pawnee Bill, the cowboy Tom Mix, and, eventually, Buffalo Bill.

He'd started early with fudge. Writing to his brother in 1965, *I don't suppose you recall when I was in the Laboratory at Swifts here in Chicago, and used to make fudge in my spare time. Of course, money was scarce, so it was a case of "cadge everything one could," so I used to get the sugar by charging the refinery with my regular orders. For a long time, I bought the milk but finally figured that for free, too. I wrote the same sort of department order, and charged it to the same place with the notation "milk for the cats." That worked fine and gave me fresh milk every day until someone noticed that "milk for cats" and appeared all of a sudden with a handful of orders, saying "Let me see all those cats." I had never once thought that the government inspectors would not permit a cat around the refinery; I was caught dead to rights. The upshot was that the factory then got orders to mix soap powder with the sugar. It made it completely unsuitable for fudge, and the entire project fell by the wayside.*

I'll bet there was another project waiting in the wings.

Frank's letters, his stories, and his life teemed with dogs. When his daughters were young, the family had two German shepherds, Torf and Shebang, during the time of the heroic canine movie star Rin Tin Tin, when German shepherds were really something to have. A somber reference book, much read and inscribed in my grandfather's hand, still stands on my bookshelf. In later life, there was always a dog in the house—Morgan, Sandy, Pepsi—but none that I remember had any purpose. Not so in Fort Worth.

We used to have a flock of dogs, each a specialist in his own right. One would be a coon dog, another for possums, one for rabbits, another for squirrels, another a bird dog, and on and on. No matter what sort of game jumped up ahead of us we were well prepared and had the dog for the occasion.

We became imbued with the idea of being "trainers" and accumulated all these dogs—a grand assortment, all sizes, shapes, ages, breeds, colors that you can imagine. Collectively, they totaled 27 in number.

Our method of training was unorthodox to say the least. I remember a bird dog which persisted in chasing rabbits, much to my father's disgust. I boasted I could break him of that, so JW said "okay, he is yours. I want no more of him." I started my training session with a short barreled shot gun (the barrel was short because some kid and I tried to shoot a cleaning rag out of it) and when the first rabbit came up, old King took out after him. I blazed away with one barrel and then the other and King came tearing back to me, well peppered with bird shot and very contrite. From that day on, he lost all interest in rabbits. In fact he even forgot he was a dog. He never hunted a single thing after that, was underfoot all the time. He just wouldn't get out in front!

We even had a special trading dog. He always went hunting with us, and when the marksmanship wasn't too good or we just hadn't seen anything to shoot, we'd stop at Tipton's country store to get something to eat. . . . When we hadn't killed any game, we'd trade Big Dog for cheese and crackers, or sardines. The storekeeper would tie Big Dog with a rope, and after many sad farewells we'd bid him goodbye and start for home. Upon our arrival, there would be Big Dog on the porch awaiting us with a length of rope attached to his collar. We loved to think he was such a friend that nothing could keep us apart. We did learn in later years that Mr. Tipton always sent a bill to our dad for the food he supplied.

All four boys grew up to lead long, self-sufficient, and opinionated lives. Frank's bent for independent thinking and entrepreneurial action did not fade as he grew into adulthood—I've seen traces of work running a rendering operation for Swift and Company in Memphis, as a newspaper advertising model (trustworthy businessman), a distributor for punch card games, the co-owner of an auto garage, and the designer and builder of the Baby Safe Table, one of which still resides in our basement. Some of his letters are written on stationery marked Baby-Safe Division, Condon Industries. There were, to my knowledge, no other divisions. His brother Tex stayed in the cattle business, as a commission man and then a widely known auctioneer, traveling all over the West starting in the 1930s in his own small plane. On the side was painted "TEX" CONDON, THE BIG BULL SHIPPER. Next-in-line Bob worked for Tex his whole life, and the youngest, Charles, settled in Sioux City, Iowa, got into the trucking business, and as years went by would refer proudly to the proliferation of Condons in the city phone directories.

When I think of the things we did as kids I really wonder that we all lived to manhood. If today's kids did the things we did, there would be congressional investigations, programs for the underprivileged and planned activity for every minute. They would not have an opportunity to have any time for themselves at all. I don't feel that we ever missed a thing—to live it all over again I wouldn't change a thing. I think the world would be better off if we could all go back to the time we knew as kids.

There is in Frankie's letters a sense of cheerful mortality, particularly in the years before his death. He refers to the future as a time "after I've gone to California," which in his dry Texas boyhood must have seemed a green and verdant wonderland. He and his brothers, he reports, "are living on borrowed time" at their ages. He mentions the Old Gent with the Big Scythe. He reports his own increasingly frequent visits to the hospital with equanimity, resilience, and humor. A plain postcard (five cents) in 1971 declares, with his caps and a center-justified title:

TWO DOWN—ONE MORE TO GO

(visits to MEMORIAL HOSPITAL, St. Joseph).

Now back home again after 9 days as pneumonia patient and feeling better by the hour.

Hoping for comparable good luck on THIRD DOWN.

Education on OXYGEN, INHALATION THERAPY, ETC now practically complete, nothing more necessary or desired so hold flowers.

There are a few Texas artifacts still in the house on Lake Michigan. Photos of the family by various spare-looking houses and of the boys seated on burros. Landscape shots from around Fort Worth and around the stockyards, which makes me wonder who had the photographic impulse. Several spurs. A longhorn rack. Curiously, a trio of felt booster banners that may have once waved at football games: Mineral Wells, Fort Worth, San Antonio. My brothers have the guns: a .22 and a .38-caliber six-shooter bought around 1905 at the famous gunmaker A. J. Anderson on Houston Street in Fort Worth.

Before I left the family nest and flew off into the world, I remember my grandfather downstairs in the lake bedroom, hunched over the battered and antiquated typewriter, hunting and pecking and overusing the carbon ribbons, waiting to be served his lunch by the women of the house. I doubt I ever asked him what he was doing. He was writing his memories to someone I never knew, someone who saved them in a shoebox. A year after his death, the kind stranger sent them back, and there they sat in their manila envelope for thirty years until they came to me, Frankie's letters from *that country*.

(2011)

Uncle Tex's Wedding

St. Paul Dispatch, June 19, 1919.

HORSEMAN DASHES INTO HOTEL, SEIZES
BRIDEGROOM.

A horseman last night spurred his steed through
the door and into the lobby of the Foley Hotel,
Seventh and Jackson Streets, while a reception in
honor of Mr. and Mrs. John William Condon,
married at the St. Paul Cathedral yesterday
morning, was in progress.

The horseman headed his mount directly towards
the bride. Her husband quickly stepped between
them to shield her from the invader. Not to be
outwitted, the lone rider caught Condon in his
grasp, swung his horse about, and rider and victim
disappeared though the door.

Men in the lobby rushed to prevent the abduction,
but were forced to retreat by a volley of shots from
more than fifty revolvers, grimly grasped by an
equal number of horsemen waiting outside.

While the intruders held the would-be rescuers at a
distance, Condon, despite his vehement protests,
was tied securely to a hayrack. The vehicle, with its
cortege of shooting, howling horsemen, started up
the street, a source of wonder to pedestrians.

You can learn so much from family history. Our ancestors
are not stiffly posed, elaborately hatted cardboard cutouts,
no matter what the pictures look like. They were people!

And some of them were like my great uncle Tex Condon, abducted from his own wedding reception by shooting, howling horsemen, ninety years ago this very day in the streets of decorous downtown St. Paul.

The bride was a very young society girl, just graduated from convent school, whose father owned the hotel that was the site of the shenanigans. Tex was a cattleman from the South St. Paul stockyards, and it was members of their notorious booster club, Hook 'Em Cow, who rousted the 250 well-dressed guests from their civilized celebration and took their pal Tex for what the paper called a "careening ride around town."

You just have to wonder what the new in-laws were thinking as the hayrack and the horsemen disappeared down the street.

Tonight is the ninetieth anniversary of my great uncle Tex's (first!) wedding, and my sister and I intend to dine in the old Livestock Exchange Building in South St. Paul, where he no doubt did business, and then drive up Concord Street, imagining fifty boisterous Hook 'Em Cow boys, full of purpose and mischief, trotting on a hot afternoon up toward the city, where the unsuspecting young couple was receiving in a ballroom decked with ferns and white peonies. Maybe we'll carry a peony or two ourselves in honor of the story, and of Great Uncle Tex's wedding.

(2017)

The Rings

Twenty-five years in, I wear four rings now, stacked closely on my ring finger, an untraditional presentation in a traditional order. The wedding ring closest, with its hidden engraving, and next the engagement ring with a row of tiny diamonds set into the gold. Another channeled ring of ten larger stones, for the ten-year anniversary. And for twenty, alternating birthstones for the four of us . . . two diamonds for Doc and daughter Maggie, the Aprils, and two aquamarines for the Marches, son John and me. Four birthdays in five weeks; at the farm, we had a special cake-and-candles flag and just let it fly the whole time.

Doc had a friend in the jewelry business, a client of course, named Mimi. He would remember her pets' names, too, and their medical histories, but I don't. I'd said that I didn't want a ring with a stone that would stick up; I had some sense that it would be a trouble with winter gloves, or maybe backstage when I was working. We must have gone to look at something, to pick it out, but I hardly remember that part. In some ways, he is a very traditional man, and it was as if we were pretending we just happened to be in the jewelry store browsing. I must have been content to go along. The store I remember was in a place called Bandana Square in St. Paul, and it was a renovated, rebuilt old roundhouse. There was a train museum in there, and the developer was trying to fill it with upscale shops. The jewelry store was one of those.

I remember the moment when the decision was made, though. I had just turned thirty-four, and he was just turning thirty-six. (Some months later, some shopkeeper referred to me as a "mature" bride.) We were at my place, the little jewel box house on Twenty-Second Avenue, and I was flopped on the bed. We'd been dating for a couple of years. It was probably a Monday, which was the only day we really had any time together—my day off at the theater— and probably at night after Doc finished at the clinic. (Because of our wildly opposing schedules, we functioned for a long time as two successful professional people who slept together. Monday evenings were just about it, or time after midnight when my shows were over. Occasionally, we'd go somewhere for a couple of days. He had come to see me in Denver at the theater; I'd gone along on a field trial or two. We were sampling each other's lives, looking at each other in our own contexts, without much melding. My friend Sally has said, "there's nothing sexier than talent." We were both very talented.) And I remember saying, without any preparation and a little absently, "I think I might be ready for a baby." And he said, without a pause, "I'm ready, too." And so it was done.

But. Before that.

We started dating after my dog nearly died. Old Vagabond had been the companion of my theater travels for nearly ten years, having been a happy Indiana farm stray in danger of being executed by the local hunt to keep him out of the foxhounds. When I'd left the area, he'd been ambling through the yard. I opened the back door and said "jump in," and he did. He'd lived in Minneapolis, in Colorado, in Arizona, in my houses and in those of my sequential boyfriends. If he needed vet care, I called Dr. Baillie back in Minnesota, and when I settled in south Minneapolis and bought a house, the clinic was conveniently up the street. I was in my first flush at the Guthrie Theater, closing shows, opening them, rehearsing six out of seven days, but Vagabond had no sense of timing. He fell ill the day before I was due to open *Peer Gynt*, in a challenging modern production directed by a Romanian and lit by a famous New York designer. It would be a fifteen-hour day for sure. I arrived at the clinic in the early morning, my heavy dog draped in my arms, barely breathing, and left him. In my pocket was a phone number: "Call me here when you're done with the show."

It was after midnight when I made the call, and I could hear a party in the background. Someone called Dr. Baillie to the phone, and he said simply, "Meet me at the clinic." Filled with dread, I left the bright theater and drove through the cold. He met me at the front door and locked it behind me; the lights were off in the front and on in the back, and I followed him into the kennels, expecting a sheeted body and a farewell. He bent over something in the back, and there was a metallic click. The kennel door swung open, and out walked my dog, a little tentative but headed right for my hand and embrace.

And afterward, we took the dog out the back door of the clinic into the quiet alley. There was a light snow falling, picked up by the streetlight. We stood there a moment. We might have looked right at each other. It was done.

That was in early January. By March, I had introduced Doc to my work—"I haven't been to a play since college"—and he had started willingly enough on what turned out to be a solid twenty-five years of accompanying me to the theater. He had quit on the girl who'd been waiting at the party. It had gotten around the theater bar that I was dating someone outside the profession. The actresses were agog.

I'd let my college horse go a few years before, my beautiful, witless Saddlebred mare, sold for her breeding and not to ride. I still had all my gear, though, and my horse habits, learned in early formal forward-seat training—think hard hats and jodhpurs, little boots and a crop—and from teaching saddle seat in college. There were, I knew, certain ways to handle your horses, certain ways to mount and ride, certain good safety rules and protocols, and a person's love for the creatures and their dusty good smells and inquisitive ears should be contained in the framework of what you did and what you didn't do, both to and with your horses.

Doc asked me to come out to his farm to ride one day that was either late winter or early spring, however you describe a Minnesota day when there is sun, thin sun, but the ice is still rimming the ponds and the landscape is all grays and browns. We saddled up two of his Tennessee Walkers with gear unfamiliar to me—a hard-seated flattish saddle with stiff leather stirrups, breastplates, long-bitted bridles. Doc's saddlebags were stamped with his initials. He wore quite a hat.

It was low country that would be marshy in the thawed months, crisscrossed by gravel roads set above the dead reeds and grasses that rustled in the wind. We rode a distance; I quite liked the Walkers, with their rapid, willing gait and ground-covering comfort. I could see why they were the favorites for following big-running competition dogs in a field. Mine was Mishak, on the small side, very smooth and comfortable, steady and alert to his surroundings and to me. He and Red Man moved like a team along the road, warming with exertion, and Doc and I held hands as we went.

Until we cut across the bog. "Shortcut back," my future husband announced cheerily as he plunged Red Man into the ditch and into the water and ice. Accustomed as I was to arenas and box stalls and equitation classes, I reined up for a minute, but the horses took the new terrain serenely. The footing seemed all right. I pulled my boots above the waterline and took a stronger grip with my thighs, giving Mishak more rein to negotiate the hidden bottom. The wise creature pricked his ears forward in attention, looking hard and following big Red Man, who was creating quite a wake in icy water above his knees. Doc looked over his shoulder and smiled at me, and I smiled back. I saw Red Man hesitate, then hunch back and hop. Some kind of underwater obstruction that he'd chosen to lift over. A moment later, Mishak and I were at the same spot, and there we stopped.

The horse was nobody's fool. When his forward motion caught, he rocked back and tried again. His attention went out of his ears and head and down into his legs and hooves as he considered the situation, shifted his weight, strained a moment, and then settled. No fear, no distress, but recognition. This was a situation beyond his power; this was something up to the human.

I gave the good fellow a pat and a reassuring word and

looked down into the water. He seemed to be standing off a
little bit, not quite foursquare. Up ahead, Doc and Red Man
splashed up out of the marsh and onto the roadbed and
turned. "Try him again," he called, and I did, with my voice
and my hands, but the horse was smarter than we were. He
stood, steam rising off his sweated neck and ice floating
around his submerged legs. And I started to think about all
the careful care I'd been taught to administer to horses over
the years, how many hours I'd walked hot horses until they
were cool and dry, how many warm baths, how many leg
bandages.

I slipped off the horse into the water, thigh-deep and cold,
stepped forward a few paces through the sucking mud
bottom, and tried to lead him. He started and stopped. I
came close and ran my hands down his front legs into the
water, trying to feel what was holding him. He stood and
waited. Up on the road, Doc dismounted and put Red Man
to a ground tie, dropping the reins to the gravel. *Why*, I
thought distractedly, *would he ever stay there?* The wind was
coming up. The dead grasses were rustling. There was no
house as far as I could see.

Doc spoke to Mishak as he waded toward us and then
leaned over, plunging his arms deeply into the water around
his back legs. "Well, he's caught," he said, standing up.
"Log or something down there." We stood there for a
minute, and I started to imagine a rescue operation. One of
us would have to stay with the horse. The other would go
for a truck and men, maybe a winch or a saw. And a
blanket. We'd need a blanket to throw over wet, hot Mishak
before he became wet, cold Mishak. And when we got him
back to the farm, he'd need a warm mash and to be rubbed

down hard. I wondered if there was a laceration somewhere that we couldn't see, blood flow slowed by the cold water and mud.

And while I was thinking that, Doc started to strip the saddle and breastplate off the horse, the leathers cold and stiff, the sheepskin wet and warm. He waded over and laid them on top of a nearby tussock of grass, out of the water. "What are you doing?" I asked him. "I'm going to roll him over."

I was appalled. No horse I'd ever heard of or imagined would stand for being laid down, head sinking toward the water, and rolled belly up and over, without struggling. And struggling at close quarters with a fearful eleven-hundred-pound animal while standing in thigh-deep icy water, although it had never come up specifically in my lessons, seemed to be exactly the kind of situation my training had taught me to avoid. Now my mental rescue operation included my dragging my soaked and injured date out of the water and onto the road, covering him with my jacket, catching Red Man, and then riding like hell for help. I wondered which way was the nearest house.

But that's what he did. While I stood off and held the reins, Doc reached down and pulled up a back leg until the horse went down, and levered him over sideways into the muck, which allowed Mishak to free his hock from the underwater log, and when he came all the way over—and I think the horse was helping now—he lurched to his feet in new water, with new ground, the log left behind. "Take him out," Doc said, and I turned toward the road and took a step, but Mishak had the same good idea. He passed me in a series of little leaps through the mud and water, and I floundered after him, running and staggering, until we climbed up to the road and stood, both panting and streaming water to the gravel.

A half hour later, I was the one in the warm bath at the farm, with my future husband and two plastic glasses of brandy, while Mishak stood in the shed, lipping his feed. He cooled out nicely on the ride home, had one visible cut which was quickly treated, showed no sign of lameness or upset. We were the ones who were cold and wet and needed warm blankets, a remedy we were happy to apply to ourselves.

We went to the Lexington for the big meet-his-family dinner. Prime rib all around, and brandy alexanders made with real ice cream. I was dressed in something nice, and I remember that Doc was wearing—brace yourself—a pale powder-blue suit, and it looked even paler in contrast to his usual black cowboy boots, which later would make an appearance at our wedding, but would look better polished up, with a tux. And we were sitting at a round table and were only partway through our polite and happy meal when the maître d' brought a phone tableside. With a long cord, because this was the eighties. Maybe that explains the powder blue, too. There was a phone call for Dr. Baillie.

Doc was still running championship field dogs at that time, and his favorite bitch was whelping that night. She was at the clinic, and someone was watching, but she wasn't doing well. Five minutes later we were in the truck and on the way, and in fifteen minutes we were going in the back door, and ten minutes after that I was standing at the foot of an operating table and the anesthetized Veeta was spraddled out on her back and I was helping by holding her legs wide apart to extend the belly for the scalpel. Her skin was stretched and taut, and it seemed briefly like a scene from Kafka. Doc had put a mask over his beard but hadn't even stopped to take off his jacket. He looked up, and I could see him smiling through the mask. "You might want to look away while I make the incision," he said. And I held her legs apart, and I did look away. He took five strong puppies out of her and closed her with quick, confident stitches, at which point I started looking again. She lay on her side, sleeping and loose, until she shook off the anesthetic, opened her eyes, and sprang to her feet in one movement, looking around for the babies.

The blood got all over the pale blue suit, and Doc had a little explaining to do when he took it to the dry cleaner—"I'm a *veterinarian*," he said patiently and several times over—but it never really came out. I could always see the long-shadowed splotches down the pant legs and on the skirts of the jacket. He was never a powder-blue suit kind of guy anyway.

Some people are illuminated by their work. There's nothing so sexy as talent. I had always liked veterinarians.

We were married at the Calhoun Beach Club, by my old Chicago friend Judge Margaret O'Malley and a Minnesota judge who had to be there for it to be legal. I don't even remember his name. We were married in December, in a room all lit with crystal and white and shine, full of representatives from our various communities. I wore a dress built for me in the Guthrie costume shop, intricate lace like snow falling and a close ribbon around my neck.

Any wedding is experienced in revelatory flashes.

Beforehand, standing on the balcony of the top-floor suite, looking over the icy lake at a red winter sunset, and our friends arriving, small, below.

The chorus of the Gershwin song we used as a processional. *I was above love, before, but now I love love, because you're, oh oh so nice*, which perfectly expressed the reason I married.

I hated the idea of being given away, and there was nobody to do that anyway, so he met me at the bottom of the long stairway, and we processed together up to the dais while one of the actresses sang. It was, someone told me later in my blur, the most intelligent wedding processional they'd ever seen.

We stayed in the upstairs suite that night, and in the morning the dress and tux were strewn about on the furniture. We changed into traveling clothes and headed for the airport and London.

A couple of years after the soaked horses and the puppy-saving surgery, but long before we started celebrating anniversaries, ten, twenty, and twenty-five, we picked up the ring, still in that not-discussing-it, just-happen-to-be-here mode, and walked out of the store and into the parking lot. Doc suddenly took me into his arms and leaned me up against the car, or more probably the truck, took the little box out of his pocket, and said, "I can't wait another minute. Will you marry me?"

(2009)

Verse III

RAISING CHILDREN

Die Hard with a Vegetarian

My son John is turning into a wonderful reader. Pages with one-syllable words and a big illustration are only amusing artifacts to him now; chapter books and big words hold complete sway. He's at a bold stage, curious about the story and eager to find out what will come next. So he concentrates on the overall idea, jumping over anything he doesn't recognize or just improvising. He's been taught inventive spelling, and now, he's an inventive reader.

We practice on grocery lists and maps, cereal boxes and license plates. He reads street signs, helping me search for addresses. Reading, he has discovered, is not just a matter of storybooks. It's useful, and it carries information that he wants. The world is full of toy catalogs and television schedules. Soon, we hope, it will be full of newspapers and award-winning children's novels. And of course, there are the movie listings.

On movie nights, it is John's job to read me the list of possibilities as we drive toward the cash machine. Some he has already heard about in school, I shudder to report, which is why he has always been able to recognize titles like *Species* and *Mortal Kombat* and reads them faultlessly, with a hopeful little glance in my direction. Not likely, honey.

Others, with long or unfamiliar words, are read more, well, imaginatively. Or ingeniously. Or perhaps the right word is *ingenuously*.

"All right," he'll say, briskly opening the paper, "how about *The Bridges of Madder Country*? Or here's something called *Flittering with Disaster*"—the word *disaster* always sounds promising to little boys—and the copy says it is "exciting and wildly organ-l." What, he wants to know, is the story of the movie called *Dr. Jerky and Mr. Hyde*? Or this one sounds attractively spooky: *Jane Eerie*.

John always spends a little time searching through the display ads for movies I did not let him see before, in the hope that I will have weakened. He particularly likes one that looks like it has really big explosions: *Die Hard with a Vegetarian*.

He's doing great, and we're really proud of him. The child has no fear of syntax and understands what he should— that reading carries information and that words are there to be read boldly. We've added the Family Events portion of the paper to John's reading, so this is our newspaper-based outing plan for this weekend. We'll go see that well-known Steve Martin movie *Sergeant Blinko*, and then follow it up with a trip to St. Paul for a ride on John's favorite amusement machine. You know the one, with the wooden horses that go up and down. It's listed under Community Attractions as the "Casserole."

(1996)

Wanting Hot Lunch

Maggie wants hot lunch. She is tired of peanut butter sandwiches, even when they have honey in them. Red Jell-O hearts are no longer interesting; juice boxes kept carefully cool, cups of applesauce, even goldfish crackers have palled. At seven, her palate is fatigued. She requires more, well, stimulation at noon. In respite from the rigors of second grade, she longs to march with the other kids through the cafeteria line, picking up a napkin and a spork, controlling her own destiny. Choosing her own dessert.

What are her tools? We are currently discouraging demands and tantrums and encouraging creative problem-solving, the use of sweet reason, and reading skills. Hence, Maggie's new approach. On the arrival of the school menu in the come-home folder—an event which I view as an unscrupulous marketing tool by unseen hot lunch forces—she reads it, with enthusiasm, using every bit of her considerable creativity and demonstrating laudable courage in the face of new words. "Cheese pizza" and "mini corn dog" present no challenge, but . . . Salisbury steak?

But not for nothing have we been encouraging her toward the literary arts for seven years, stumbles and all. When she finds an entrée she does not recognize, she charges forward anyway, reading the word just as if she knew what it was.

The results, frankly, leave me with renewed enthusiasm for peanut butter sandwiches with a side of Oreos. Because the other kids, apparently, are having rice with chicken chow "mean." "Cheeser" salad. And every day, she tells me enthusiastically, they have "desert"!

Struggling to keep the car on the road, murmuring supportively, and making no corrections, I ponder a lunch that features a potato bar with "aspirated" toppings. That would be assorted toppings, I hasten to clarify, dear reader. And I wonder at what point in the curriculum the concept of abbreviations is introduced. The school menu is printed in a calendar format, and space is limited. That must be why Maggie wants hot lunch on the day when the featured dessert is "choc" cake. She does not think she is interested in "tropical pud."

In Italian, or "italan" fare, she favors spaghetti and wonders what "cheese troutalina" could be. I wonder, too; it's tortellini. And when she comes to that Salisbury steak, what comes out is "celebrity steek."

I believe we'll just go on with cream cheese and jelly, baby carrots, and the occasional tuna salad. I'm hoping to keep her from one bit of line blurring between at-home food and school food, and consequently rushed her by the freezer in the grocery store this week, distracting her with some bit of motherly byplay. I was afraid she'd notice, in the freezer and on sale, one of the foods she most frequently asks about from the school lunch menu. We could have it at home: how about some "tater toots"?

(1997)

Mothering Boys

I never imagined myself as the mother of an eight-year-old boy.

Oh, I've gotten used to young children. I face preschool classes unafraid, am the first one there for running noses, skinned knees, problems with sharing, and encounters with Scary Things.

Solomon is not wiser, Mother Teresa no more patient, the Madonna herself no more adoring. No child goes unnoticed; no small triumph unapplauded. I mean this. I love them. I hope these are abilities and joys that I will keep for the rest of my life.

But life is moving on. I think I need some new skills.

What, for example, is the correct response to this? We're window-shopping on vacation, in an upscale little resort town by the water. My son is dashing ahead up the street when he stops to look in the window of a pricey women's shop. He turns and yells through the crowd, waving his arms happily. "Hey, Mom, come look at this! This would make a great Sex Dress for you!" It creates something of a stir.

Or the response to this? "Lauren says James is fat, but I know he's not fat! He's just really strong. But Lauren says he can't play the game on days when she's boss because he's fat."

Or this? "Mom, Señora got mad at me because I didn't know the world for *pear* or *banana*. But that was when I was home sick. She always gets mad at the boys when we've been sick and missed class, but she never gets mad at the girls. I don't like her. It's not fair."

I've thought for years, eight to be exact, that parents, not corporate executives, are the ones who deserve to have research departments and staff advisers. We need them more; we make hundreds of influential decisions each week and usually on six hours of sleep a night.

Shelves of parenting books are no good; we need the accumulated wisdom of the ages on tap, available in an instant. And even that may not help you grapple with this beloved, and strange, creature that your nine-pound baby has become. He can seem loud, unbelievably loud. Gross, unrelievedly gross. And often bewilderingly different from you.

One night a year or so ago I said helplessly, and a little angrily, to my husband that I hoped he was ready to deal with this. Like many women, I'm not entirely comfortable with some of the terrain in boy country, being constitutionally unattracted to explosions and belligerent facemaking. I don't really want to know more about the Megazords than I already do; I don't care to sport shoot or take up ice hockey. Our interests are, to some extent, diverging.

But whether I am wise or not, well advised or not, our growing son is traveling toward the male territory—a place that will be important and formative to him, where I am only an observer. Having learned babies and toddlers, I am now learning boy, thinking ahead with some trepidation toward mothering an eleven-year-old, a teenager.

It is necessary to work to disregard the stereotypes, and it is not made easier by the fact that some of them are true. If I don't want him to go on entirely without me, I need to look at his world more clearly, more tolerantly, and more lovingly.

No doubt we'll have our divergences. He recently told his teacher his all-time favorite book is something called "It's Morphin' Time"—and after all those Oz books, too. But with attention and thought, I can see there are recognizable landmarks for my son and for me, in his future as a middle-sized boy and mine as his mother.

Is he loud? Definitely yes. Gross? Sometimes. And also . . .

He is fiercely loyal to his friends. ("I got kneed in the groin today and had to go to the nurse's office, and I have to call Tommy right away because Mrs. Flanagan thought he did it on purpose and I know it was an accident, but I couldn't tell her because I was crying so hard.")

Once they trust you, eight-year-old boys, and their friends, want to show you things—origami cranes and string games, special rocks and broken toenails.

They wonder about the world and are funny beyond belief. They rap to themselves in the mirror and spike their hair in the bathtub. They have big, big plans.

What is he proud of? Learning to ride a horse fast. And a million other things. What is he afraid of? That the other kids will find out he needs help with spelling.

What ideas will we have in common as he grows into a man and I remain a woman and we become friends as well as relatives? Kindness (Lauren and fat James) and fairness (what about Señora's getting mad at the boys?). Justice, the future, curiosity, spirituality, travel, animals, books. Trust.

And ten million other things. I don't need to bone up on the various classifications of attack helicopters. We can both enjoy that he knows something I don't. Boy country is still on the same sphere as mine, and we are closely linked with love.

(1994)

Verse IV

CIVIC DISCOURSE

You're the Favorite Flag

I've had a lot of occasion to think about the flag lately, since our daughter has made up her song about it. With that sweet, steely determination that very young children can have, she starts singing every time she sees the flag, regardless of the pained expression of her brother, who covers his ears vigorously and mutters as long as it goes on.

"Old Glory," she warbles loudly, "you're my favorite flag. You're the favorite flag of John's and mine" (here a particularly loud groan from her brother).

Every sight of Old Glory is treated in this celebratory if tuneless fashion. If there is a row of flags at a car dealership, Maggie happily starts over every time she catches sight of another one. She punches up the opening for emphasis, like any performer.

It is the beauty of the flag that delights her, I think, with its bright colors and fluttery gladness. She sang and sang at a town parade recently, despite a cold wind that whipped off the lake. But it was little John who, suddenly quiet, asked about the other flags. "Mom," he said, "are those the flags for the lost GI Joes? Should we stand up?"

In silence, even gravely, two rows of women and men were carrying POW/MIA flags. Each black flag with its silhouetted profile had two red streamers hung from the top of its pole. The flags represent Minnesota's forty-two lost "GI Joes," the POW/MIAs in Southeast Asia.

My daughter singing and my little son solemn. The wind off the lake and the sounds of the approaching marching bands. And the volunteers walking by, carrying black flags with the names of the absent. It was a moment to think about.

And what it makes me think about are the people carrying the flags, marching along in the parade. They represent, I think, the best hope for our difficult country, troubled as it is by currents of discord and confusion. It is not because of what they believe or don't believe; it is because they're doing something we should all be doing. They are standing up and moving.

Thinking about the public affairs of the nation—whether the topic is lost soldiers or misbehaving politicians or pork barrel construction in your own neighborhood—starts as a private matter. One mutters over the newspaper, stares at the networks, listens to the all-news radio on the way to work. This is the subterranean murmur of the people thinking, that current the pundits and politicians try so hard to hear.

The difficulty is that so much of all that fertile and various opinion stays subterranean. Somehow, for many people, it has seemed unseemly or a waste of time or even hopeless to talk about what they think. But the life of the nation does not stop because people are not speaking up. Our country is being run in that vacuum of public opinion. If you're not engaged, you are contributing to the vacuum.

We need to make it easier for our administrators to hear what we think. In fact, we need to make it *unavoidable* for them to hear what we think. They are, after all, working for us.

So, mutter over the newspaper, and then mention the

source of your mutters to a coworker. Stare at the networks, and then call them up and respond. If you think they're wasting your time with follow-up stories on Dan Quayle's spelling skills, say so. Listen to the all-news radio, and talk back.

Just stand up and move. Volunteer to pass out flyers for something you believe in. Call your local government to complain about the expansion of the gravel pit in your backyard. Drop a topic into the middle of your next barbecue. You'll be surprised at how opinionated people are and how wise they can be.

It does not matter what the topic is or where you stand on an issue. Discussions cannot be one-sided; good arguments air issues. But they have to be conducted out loud. It is necessary to take private backyard grousing about the state of the world and turn it into public discourse.

I've heard Senator Paul Wellstone speak about his belief in the power of an "aroused citizenry." That's a formal way of saying: First, get into a discussion. Then, stand up and get moving.

At the parade, the man wearing the "Bounce Sikorski" button and handing out flyers for his favorite congressional candidate is a citizen engaged in public discourse. He is, to my mind, more worthy of attention than the professionally genial politicians themselves, marching along and smiling at everyone.

The kids moving along with trash bags and picking up debris to save the environment are in the discussion, too, as are the historical society volunteers riding on their float, demonstrating their belief in learning from the past. The unsmiling men and women carrying the black flags, the families marching for this and that, even the man you've never heard of who says he is running for president, they're all speaking—and they are all standing up.

And in a nascent way, so are my children. They begin by making up a song about one flag, by asking about the solemnity of another. Never believe that children don't notice when someone stands up. Never believe they don't remember it.

It's my favorite flag, too, Maggie. Not because it is beautiful, although it is. And not because I believe in everything our country does, because I don't. It's my favorite flag because it represents people of good heart and will and wisdom and diversity of opinion. It is a citizenry that can be aroused and the best hope for our future and yours.

And yes, little John, we should stand up.

(1992)

So We Tell Them: Girl Power

It was a long parade and a perfectly clear, warm night, with people leaning back in their lawn chairs and smiling police moving children off to the side. There were the obligatory marching bands, of course, and marching politicians. We saw some clowns and a classic car or two. For all we know, there might also have been performing elephants and a B-52. There was no time to look around. In company with three other moms one night this fall, I was shepherding Girl Power down the main street of North St. Paul.

I hasten to say that it was not the kind of Girl Power that comes in slinky dresses and shoes that force you to begin every motion with your hips. This kind doesn't have hips yet and still wants sneakers because you can run in them. They're adorned with beads and bows, not sequins. Instead of satin, sashes. Not Spice Girls, Girl Scouts.

September's Heritage Days parade in North St. Paul provided the perfect circus atmosphere for our scouts, Troop 1617 from Mounds Park Academy, to loose their formidable energies on the open air and an appreciative crowd. Those we marched past laughed and waved as the girls chanted—or maybe shrieked—that famous old camp song that starts, "Everywhere we go, people want to know, who we are, so we tell them." The scout troop marching directly in front of us was, I suspect, a little less enchanted by all that shrill repetition; after the first verse, they knew who we were. Smiling over their shoulders, their leaders, too, slightly winced.

I winced myself when an official-looking video camera appeared ahead of us and chose an adorable small Brownie for an in-motion interview. Our girls, who are bigger in every sense of the word, enthusiastically charged the cameraman in an effort to "be on TV." I'm waiting for the call that tells me I appeared in the background on cable coverage of the parade, waving my arms at our girls and hissing, "Let the little one be the star!"

Having read *Reviving Ophelia* on its publication date, and hearing the many common horror stories about what can happen to girls as they grow, we're all watching for signs of self-esteem damage in our scouts. All in all, so far, we don't see a thing. In fact, on meeting days, holed up in a classroom with fifteen nine-year-old girls and trying to lead a discussion about Juliette Low, we sometimes think a little less assertiveness would be a good idea.

But that's a passing thought. As women, we know that our girls will need every scrap of scrappiness to develop their full potential. We know that the world they're growing into is not hospitable to women of deliberate intention and that much of what they will learn works against the bold buoyance of age nine. Regardless of the camp chant, the world will not necessarily want to know who they are. We hope that linking arms with other women and shouting their names into the wind is a joy they will remember as they grow, and that along with developing bodies and minds, they will develop the strength to stay on their feet and thrive.

A night of bold marching can only help. There might have been a hundred or two Girl Scouts on the street in North

St. Paul that night, all attended by women who give their time as volunteer leaders because they care about the future of their girls and, by extension, the future of all girls. Afterward, our scouts rushed some community volunteers providing cans of soda to thirsty marchers, and they flocked to surround several Community Princesses who had descended from their parade car. Perhaps those princesses were waiting for a ride, in their long gowns, tiaras, and end-of-summer tans. In the behavior of true princesses, they spoke kindly to the girls, shaking hands and allowing the girls to touch their long, satin gloves. "I like your mittens," said one of our girls in the quietest tones we'd heard all evening. Perhaps they were just kind teenagers who remembered being short and nine and thinking you would never be tall and beautiful. Or perhaps they'd been Girl Scouts, too.

So, let Troop 1617 strut and shout and love every minute of their nine-year-old lives. We are their leaders only momentarily, scurrying along behind them, trying to catch up as they dash ahead into the night and the crowd. Right now, they're chasing princesses and a cold drink. Soon, they'll be chasing their dreams into a future that belongs to them.

(1998)

Doing Some Damned Thing

Separation of church and state is an old and honorable, and permeable, division in American life. People do not leave their intellect in church cloakrooms on the Sabbath, and they are certainly enjoined to carry their moral principles back out into the weekday world, where those principles should be a framework for daily life and action.

The two are related. For one thing, passionate, political support is faith-based, in the sense that we act on a secular faith in our candidates. We have to. Their pronouncements, we all know, are tailored for our ears. We don't really know what they're going to do if they're elected. We must act on faith that their actions will resemble their promises.

And in some ways, as any church leader knows, church life is politics writ small. Rising above the fray, with a determined eye on our better selves, is part of the work, and it is not always easy.

A fevered political season makes it more difficult. On the one hand, churches are powerfully knitted community institutions, rooted in the most deeply held beliefs of their members and providing a common roof under which the congregation can stand together, observing the world and, we hope, considering it. On the other hand, any political activity inside a church imperils its nonprofit status. No politics in the pulpit, no brochures on the social hall tables, all is resolutely neutral.

This is complicated. I attend a church full of people who are politically active, and we the opinionated have been (you should forgive the expression) religious in the last year about making sure there is no political work within our doors. No support or opposition to any candidate, no tables with campaign literature. The premises are resolutely neutral.

The occupants, however, are anything but neutral, as evidenced by the boiling conversations, the passionate conferences at coffee hour, the extended parleys in the parking lot. Our Sunday-morning volume has been turned up.

The leadership of the northeast metro church I attend has been struggling with the Sunday service that will follow the election this year. Our people are deeply embroiled on many sides of the issues. We don't want resignation or even relaxation to set in when the polls close, and we certainly don't want to encourage resentment toward the winners or derision toward the losers. And surely we cannot just start sliding toward Thanksgiving as if the upheavals of these weeks had not occurred.

Some of us will be celebrating after the election, some will be discouraged, but our strong intention is to hold together across our differences, a small and sturdy circle of community within the larger public polity. We mean to hold together.

So on Sunday, November 9, we're going to do something different. We're going to honor not opinion, but involvement. We're going to encourage every person who did anything, anything at all, on any side, to support the electoral process in the last six months, to stand up and be applauded. And we're going to suspend religious education for that part of the service, so that every child and teen in the church can see that participation is honored. Participation is what matters. Being patriotic means doing some damned thing, any thing, to participate in our bumpy, uneven, democratic American life.

Here are some things, small and large, we know our members have done. The politically active among us run for office, knock doors for candidates, sit on advisory committees, donate to and volunteer for campaigns. But there are so many smaller things worthy of honor.

Anything counts, however small, for any side, with extra credit to those who are customarily politically inactive, or at least less active. Did you attend a caucus? Put up a yard sign? Donate, even a little, to a local candidate? Figure out what congressional district you're in and who's running. One mayoral candidate is your neighbor? Who are the others? Call any campaign headquarters and volunteer one hour to do anything they need. Do a little work on voter registration. Pick one issue, any issue, and find out both sides. Go to any website, for any candidate, and spend ten minutes figuring out who they are and why they are running. Ask someone you respect who they are voting for and why. Then ask someone you differ with. Discuss. Enable one person to get to the polls. Take your children with you into the voting booth so they can see that this right and privilege matters to you and lots of other people. Explain the political system to any young person or any immigrant.

I'll bet a similar list could be drawn up in any church or synagogue or mosque in Minnesota, a place where the serious-minded and the good-hearted have always held places at the political table.

Any damned thing at all, for any candidate at all, will qualify you to stand up at our church, and I hope for an extremely crowded sanctuary. But cast your imagination wider. Envision a standing crowd across our country—the crowd still full of opinion and even rancor. Beautifully tangled, wonderfully diverse. But united in having done something—any one small thing—as a part of our public life. *That* is a crowd to be part of. And to be proud of.

(2012)

Mr. Lincoln Is Asking You a Question

Young teens are deeply skeptical about enthusiasm in adults. Their own interests, in clothes or music or each other, can be positively dizzying, but adult attachments are viewed with a jaundiced eye, especially when they fall under the general rubric of education. The more fervently the adult tries to share, the more distant the students can become. The average end-of-the-year field trip can be an extended exercise in sighs, vacant looks, and adjustments of coiffure.

Not with Mrs. Conway.

Maureen Conway is a history teacher at Mounds Park Academy in St. Paul, Minnesota. She is an expressive and energetic woman who, along with several hardy colleagues, has been taking seventh-graders to Washington, DC, on a spring trip for the last eighteen years. This year, the count was forty-nine students, and the first tour stop was a grassy spot on the edge of Arlington National Cemetery. Standing right there near the idling buses, under the eyes of nineteen tagalong parent chaperones, Conway set about infecting the children with history.

She leaned in. They leaned in. An occasional passerby leaned in. "We are at Arlington National Cemetery," Conway said emphatically. "This is where you learn what it means to be an American. These people fought for you. These people died for you. Think about that."

Unabashedly and with vigor, she began what turned into four days of continuous American stories. At Arlington, the tale was of how Robert E. Lee's estate was turned into a

Union graveyard after he became a general for the Confederate Army of the South. The bodies of the first Union soldiers killed in the Civil War were buried in his wife's rose garden. They buried the bodies in the garden? Not a backpack rustled. The group stood in the presence of a true enthusiast, and true enthusiasm is highly contagious.

Young people know they are growing toward an uncertain future, and they need enthusiasm. It is a quality closely related to curiosity and energy, and those are contagions we want every generation to catch. Catching a bug for American history is very close to catching a bug for citizenship, and the nation's capital can be the best place to pick up a permanent infection.

So what are the ideas caught by these young people traveling to Washington in this particular spring, in the company of a devotee of American history?

- History can stir the heart. Actor John Wilkes Booth knew the play on stage at Ford's Theatre, so he watched for his cue and shot President Abraham Lincoln during the loudest laugh line. He then leaped from the presidential box and paused at center stage to shout "Sic semper tyrannis!" *Thus be it always for tyrants.* As Booth galloped away on a horse that had been held by a stagehand, Lincoln had begun to die. He was carried across the street and laid in a boardinghouse bed. Mrs. Conway showed us the theater, the presidential box, and the bed.
- The past was inhabited by people just like you. Learning "courtesies" of Colonial Williamsburg, the girls were instructed to try the manners of young women of that time and look demurely

downward when meeting a gentleman. The downcast eyes are for inspecting his calf, outstretched politely during his bow. If his calf is muscular, he may be wealthy enough to own a horse and might be a good catch. "Check him out, girls," urged the smiling guide. "Display your left hand so he can see you are not married."

- History is personal. The school's tour bus driver pointed to photos in a special display at Arlington's Women's Memorial. His eleven-year-old nephew, round-faced in his school picture, was aboard Flight 77 and died when it crashed into the Pentagon on 9/11. He had won an academic award at his school, his uncle said; the prize was a trip to California. The tour bus had just driven by the Pentagon; repairs were nearly finished.

- Your own families are part of history. One girl found her last name on the Vietnam Veterans Memorial and made a rubbing to take home. One of the parents searched the wall for the name of a young man from her hometown. In college, she'd worn a POW/MIA bracelet with his name on it. Her mother and the lost soldier's mother had had lunch together the previous week.

- You can be an active participant in making history. A man who once taught at Mounds Park Academy was now a senior aide to Senator Tom Daschle. Following the aide, the students poured through security, up to the senate majority leader's office, and out onto his section of the portico. From there, they could see the National Mall, which

stretched away below toward the Washington
Monument. The former Mounds Park teacher
answered their questions, smiling. A genial and
assured Senator Daschle stepped out to greet us.
His shirt was blindingly white. He said he hoped
we were enjoying our time in Washington. We
were.

In teachers like Conway and in all adults who brave the
bored demeanor of teens to reveal their passionate interests,
young people see a glimpse of an adult future that includes
strong interests, intellectual curiosity, and a passionate
attachment to ideas. A future like that cannot possibly be
dull or hopeless.

Maureen Conway loves monuments and memorials. She
reads the chiseled words aloud to her students, and she
teaches a special way of approaching the Lincoln Memorial.
Start at the bottom of the steps in the center, she says, and
don't look up while you climb. Don't look up until you get
to the very top step, and when you do, Lincoln will be
looking right at you. And he'll be asking you this question:
What are you going to do for this country? Don't look for
somebody else to do something. It is your job to be a
citizen, to think and vote and act. That is why Lincoln is
looking right at you and asking, *What are you going to do for
your country?*

(2002)

Talking to Teens

I left my son sitting in a public waiting area the other night. He was tired with that customary thirteen-year-old tiredness. I could see him through the restaurant window while I ordered up the egg rolls; he was wearing big jeans, Vans, a T-shirt, and a ball cap.

Coming out, I passed a security guard standing nearby. My son was now slumped deep in his chair, hat pulled low. "That guy was watching me," he said. "He thought I was going to do something bad." I looked around; the guard was gone.

I gave my son the customary maternal lecture and pep talk. If you think the guard was watching you, speak up! Tell him that you're waiting for your mom; make eye contact, pull your cap back. He might have thought you were homeless, or in trouble, or needed help.

It was a good speech, all true. But, thinking about it, I should have gone after the security guard, too.

I wonder how long he stood there looking at my son, slumped down in his chair and holding still. Couldn't he have said hello? Couldn't he have asked if the boy was waiting for someone? The words of the homily could be nearly identical. If you think the kid is in trouble or is about to make trouble, speak up! If you can't manage friendly, then for heaven's sake, be civil. Speak. Speak!

People can be terribly rude to teens, routinely exhibiting behavior that other adults would never tolerate. Watch and you'll see it every day. Adults can be dismissive and curt, or walk in front of kids as they stand looking in shop windows. We cut in front in the crowd headed toward the movie ticket booth; we interrupt them. We glare at them in their cars with the blaring music.

It can be a loud, clear message to kids, unmistakable even if unintentional: You don't matter. I'm not interested. You are not worth my consideration.

They're right. We are dissing them.

The saying goes, "if you want peace, work for justice." Couldn't we also work for courtesy? Each moment of courteous contact with young people, particularly from strangers, is a moment that reminds them they are part of a larger society and, more importantly, that society can be civil and reasonable.

A moment of civil discourse with a stranger is part of what makes a community, smoothing our daily transactions and providing over time a recognizable framework for good will. Repetitions, however casual, may even move us toward being neighbors.

It is a small stitch, but the fabric it weaves is part of what holds us all together. We exclude young people from that structure at our peril.

Make a moment of eye contact with the teen in the fast-food drive-through window. Try a hello and a real smile to the one taking your gas money, the one with the pierced tongue. Nod to the kid next to you at the stoplight. Wave to the one who yields at the intersection. Compliment the one who gives good service at the hardware store. Try a remark or two with the one carrying out your groceries, even if his hair is green.

Some teens will, of course, react as if you were an alien. You will have an occasional unpleasant moment, which will make you think automatically, *What a lout! He/she is looking at me as if I were a fogey! A crone! Me!*

This is perfectly natural. To them, in some ways, adults *are* aliens. So, make a few mental arrangements with yourself. Start by abandoning your dignity. Be willing, occasionally, to look foolish in a good cause. You cannot operate from a desire to be accepted or to be cool, no matter how clearly you remember being a teen yourself.

You are not cool now. You are an adult.

You must not be discouraged by the occasional awkward moment or even a surly response. One of the benefits of fogeyhood is the ability to rise serenely above small irritations, or at least to recognize that ability as an ideal. You'll have the small knowledge that you are improving the day and perhaps even the future.

And every once in a while, you will receive something immediate. Every once in a while, a young person treated respectfully by an adult outside their family will look up, startled at the courtesy, and catch your eye and grin.

And then, for an instant, you can see what their mothers see. Their childhood is still present in their eyes, with all its laughter and carelessness. Look carefully, and you catch a glimpse of their present, with its daring and uncertainty. And as an adult, you can imagine some of their future, full of potential, promise, and, yes, peril.

The world is an uneasy place, and teens know it. It will be theirs soon, and they know that, too. Their strides are lengthening right now; we are shifting places. While we still have their ears, speak. And let it be a kind word.

When this piece was published, the daily newspaper hired an artist to illustrate it. The artist provided a picture of a boy slouching in a chair, in a hoodie. The boy was African-American; we are not. People make assumptions, then and now. Also, I received a note from a reader, inviting me to keep my son out of his neighborhood.

(1990, 2020)

Women and Fear and a Christmas Puppy

Well, we've got our puppy. That might help at home. I can't imagine what will help when I'm out in the world. I don't want a handgun.

In fact, I didn't want a dog either. I have had a dog. Type: bosom companion. Breed: Heinz 57 varieties. For years, he went everywhere with me, depended on me totally, waited hopefully to be petted at all hours of the day and night, frolicked on walks and vacations, gave me enormous affection, and took it. Having a husband and children now, I don't need another dog for those purposes.

But over the last year or so, I've acquired something else I didn't have before, and, unlike the husband and the children, I don't know what to do with it. That something is fear—fear of violence, for personal safety and the safety of those you love.

Women's fear is a good deal like an infectious disease with varying incubation periods. Nearly all women pick it up as a youngster or a teen, at about the time they realize that something out there can hurt them, particularly if they "misbehave" or "misthink."

When women go out in the world on their own, many learn to reduce their fears to a low-grade whisper. You walk assertively. You focus on your work, your day, living your life. You read the paper with its daily glut of horror stories for women, but you never take it personally. *It won't be me,* you think. *It just won't. I'm smart, I'm fast. This doesn't really have anything to do with me.*

But at some point, the infection becomes active. I suppose

the most direct method is by injection, when your armor is pierced by personal violence. (Here I speak in happy ignorance.) But it can happen by osmosis as well. The level of violence against women in the world rises. You read the paper, listen to the news. Books and articles are written, and you read them.

There's a particularly violent crime in your city; the press has all the details, and you do, too. The victim, it appears, was a lot like you. Then a woman is shot in a convenience store parking lot, sitting next to her six-year-old. Another is murdered by a casual intruder in her home, along with one of her children. Elsewhere, driving a minivan is apparently the woman's mistake. A carjacker attacks. She dies; her child is recovered later, "unharmed," except presumably by having seen her mother killed. These are in addition to the usual run of beatings and sexual assaults.

At luncheons, at church, women you know are starting to talk about their experiences. At some point, you realize that you probably know five women who have been raped in their lives. While thinking that over, you realize you probably know a lot more. Now you're starting to get it.

Next you start to be more cautious. You call this good sense (and so does your mother), but its real name is fear. You don't let your mind wander when you're out in public; you stay aware of the people around you. You don't take those beautiful remote paths in the parks when you're walking alone. You don't walk at night at all; the dark makes you faintly nervous.

When do you realize the fear infection has become an influential part of your life? It's the day when you happen to go into the parking ramp alone, then back out of that empty stairwell and return to the entrance to ask for an escort.

Once you have an active case, your hackles are permanently raised. To your shock, you realize that violence against women has everything to do with you. And your sister and your mother and your aunt and your daughter and your friends. And the fear stays with you everywhere you go. At a women's retreat recently, held in a lodge in the middle of a remote and otherwise deserted family camp, women paired up after dark to go to the pop machine in the next building. "Want a buddy?" they said as a matter of course. There could be someone out there.

Spurred by recent news stories of real-life women and children attacked by violent men, many women's deep-seated fears of attack seem to be rising to the surface. We're getting nervous. And those nerves, fed by real incidents and nourished by images that confuse power and violence, strength and sexuality, feed the infectious disease by fear. They can cloud real transactions between real people.

Looking out my kitchen window in the exurbs, I see a pickup pull into the yard. It is a boy-toy machine, red with lots of chrome. There are two men in the front, and I can see a rifle rack.

They are harmless, as it happens—hunters asking about access to our back property. The one I talk to is only a kid, probably twenty, and exceedingly polite. But he's a large kid, very large, and all through our brief conversation, without any thinking about it, I am automatically afraid. My adrenaline, my thoughts are racing, and I'm making mental escape plans. Not in a parking ramp, not on the street, not in a mall or in a park. In my home, with my children eating crackers in the kitchen behind me.

Is this foolish? Possibly. It is uncalled for? I'm not sure. My safety and that of my children just seems too chancy. These guys are okay. What if they weren't? What if they were drunk? What if they just looked around and decided to settle in? What would I *do*?

I bitterly resent this fear; and I resent the fact that I will have to teach it to my daughter. When I was a girl, my greatest delight was to pack a sandwich and go six blocks down to the creek for the day, alone, where I would play and think and look at the sky in solitude. Now that I'm a mother, I will never be content to allow my daughter that joy. I will be too afraid.

And, women, what does the fear teach us? Action to curb violence? Anger, and then action? Unless we examine it and grapple with it, our reaction could just as easily be cowardice, or division between people, or racism, or senseless hatred, or handguns in the home. Sisters, we'll have to think on it.

These questions sadden and anger me. They led directly to getting a dog. We put a bow around its neck and told the kids it's a Christmas puppy. It's cute and cuddly and a mess to clean up after. We'll love it, and no doubt it will love us. But the sad truth is that the dog will be more than a companion for our family. We chose a big breed with a loyal heart, and we hope it will grow into something that will back us up. Something that would buy time, if needed. Something with teeth.

(1994)

Raising Nora's Flag

When we bought the farm in 1988, I had never lived in the country and had never owned a barn. We moved in on a bright autumn day, and quite suddenly my view from the kitchen encompassed two silos and a gas pump, a large population of blue jays, and six acres of grass and creeping charlie. There was space for our children and room for my husband to yell at his dogs with impunity.

There was also a flagpole.

It stood in front of the house on the corner of the top of the hill, between an enormous pine and a precipitous drop-off to the driveway. The cement that anchored it had been shabbily finished off some years earlier, like so many things on the farm, with an unsquared square of little concrete bricks. The first year, I put in red petunias and discovered there was only an inch or so of soil. They languished.

There are a lot of things to do with an old farm in the first few years, and the flagpole just stood there for quite some time, unadorned. The rope was rotted off and, although it had been constructed so that it could be lowered to the ground, the bolts were long rusted in place. A year went by before I went out one day and whacked it around in an unscientific manner, eased it to the ground, and restrung the rope.

It was my mother who gave us the flag, pulling it out of her big car along with other presentations for the new old house. She brought a tea cart, two little chairs she'd been saving for me for years, and, wrapped inelegantly in a sheet of old plastic, rough-folded, the flag. "It's huge," she said.

"It'll look great up there." Where had it come from? "It was Nora's."

When I was a little girl, we lived in a Chicago suburb built entirely around a series of country clubs, where the street names were golf-ish and vaguely Scots: Brassie, Braeburn, Bunker, Caddy. The yard was long and deep and had enormous trees in front. Way in the back, where it was bushy and unkempt (there was no gardening in our family), you could duck down and then jump up on a pair of boards that crossed a little ditch that ran water in the spring. Scrambling up an incline, you emerged into the air and light and openness of the Illinois Central Railroad commuter line. There were probably six tracks, although it seemed like more, and across that forbidden expanse were the tops of houses where unfamiliar children lived. I didn't know anyone in that neighborhood.

Freight trains clanked by in endless parade, each car swaying a little differently, the couplings holding hands. At night, the *City of New Orleans* sped along, and in its downlit windows you could catch an occasional glimpse of an arm or a woman's hat. Each morning, commuter trains arrived from the south and stopped at our station. Every twelve minutes between 6 and 9 AM, all the fathers in town got on the trains and left for the city, leaving behind a society made up entirely of women and children.

Women drove men to the station in those days. If they were late, they came fast down our street, careening toward the station, turned an impatient left to go under the viaduct, and paused to let the departing breadwinner leap out with the inevitable briefcase and newspaper. In winter, the men wore topcoats. In the windows of the passing trains, standing or sitting, they all swayed in unison, absorbed in their papers, which were triple-folded in a curious commuter kind of way. No one conversed. No one looked up.

So, northbound, they probably never saw the southbound trains, heading from downtown out into the suburbs. When those trains stopped at the Flossmoor station, the women in station wagons drove back, slower, and waited at the end of our street. Women got off the trains, coming to work carrying string bags. Each one got into a station wagon and was driven away. Sometimes there were children in the back seat and sometimes not. But the women driving were always white; the women arriving were always black. The ladies of the suburban houses were picking up the maids. Ours was Nora.

I was a child, living a small and circumscribed life. It never crossed my mind that both drivers and passengers in those station wagons were women. As I look back now through the tunnel of years and geography, I see that they probably had more in common with each other than with the heads-of-household who had departed on the earlier trains. But gender was nothing to bond over then, at least if you were female. And color was a division so deep as to be subterranean. At least if you were a child. Or at least if you were white. Or at least if you were me.

The only black people I ever saw were the maids. There might have been an occasional handyman or gardener, but a black man, even if ruled by white women, would have been a cause of uneasiness, unless he was elderly and safe. The maids were just women, of course. It seemed natural to tell them what to do. A young housewife could do it, even a child. They appeared in the morning and disappeared at the end of the day into the viaduct and gone. I never wondered where Nora had come from or where she went.

I don't remember ever picking up Nora in our station wagon or in the big green Chrysler. She must have walked. The house wasn't far down the block, almost too close to the station for prestige, in fact, although it was large and gracious-looking.

There is much about those years that I do not remember. My father was getting worse by then and had probably begun the drug abuse that would be the proximate cause of his commitment a few years later. Life in the house was a silent, somewhat fearful affair. And life outside the house was entirely artificial. Most emotion was simply shut down. The physical state of the house, except for the two front rooms and the foyer with the fountain, reflected the systemic and deep disorder of life there. Maybe Nora just cleaned the two front rooms. No one could have cleaned up the whole thing.

I do remember bits of Nora. The bits are only visual. I do not remember ever having a conversation with her or, indeed, speaking at all. One glimpse: She made fried chicken on Thursdays (we had fish sticks on Fridays), and I remember that nothing else tasted so good. The grease bubbled in the pan around the legs and breast pieces; she might have grinned as she poked it. Maybe she was grinning at me, the solemn child, watching. There was not a lot of grinning in that house. Maybe that's why I remember it so clearly.

And I remember music. I had started piano lessons at a young age with Mrs. Salter, who taught in her home at her little grand in the front room. I was an earnest and biddable sort of student, and I liked to practice. The scales and repetitions didn't bore me. Sitting at the piano, I had my back turned to my life. It was a mechanical task that pleased my mother. My fingers were entirely under my control, and sometimes they made pleasing sounds. I could feel the music, although very distantly. I couldn't feel much at all, up close.

I have a photograph taken at one of Mrs. Salter's periodic piano parties. I must be about ten. I am wearing a white blouse and a cardigan sweater and a plaid straight skirt. I cannot tell its color, as the photo is in black and white. Seated at the piano bench, feet reaching a bit for the pedals, concentrating on my piece, I am looking hard at the open music book on the rack in front of me. My hair is in two braids. My glasses are new. The photo helps me imagine myself, remember myself, practicing. This was the way I practiced, elbows stiff, focused entirely on the page, never looking down. No intonation at all, and no pedal. *Plunk. Plunk. Plunk.*

Nora would pass in back of me while I was practicing at home, crossing through the big room with the vaulted ceiling on her way to or from the kitchen. After a while (it might have been years), I was aware that she was watching me as she went by. She was not much taller than I was. And after a while longer, she stopped one day and came into my vision and spoke to me. She said, "I don't need no music," and made a movement toward the piano stool. I got up right away and stepped back. And she sat down.

I had seen Nora seated heavily on a kitchen chair from time to time, legs splayed out, resting, particularly after scrubbing the linoleum with the brush and pail. But I had never seen her sitting down anywhere else.

She looked up at me sideways, her dark hands poised over the keys. And she played. She didn't need no music, and she watched her hands. They made music that was rollicking and full and loud and involved a lot of chords rolling way up and way down the keyboard. It had a beat and lots of pedal that made it all kind of run together, unconstrained. It was nothing at all like Mrs. Salter or the piano parties.

I don't know what Nora saw when she looked up at me from the piano and her hands. She stopped, though, and quickly. She went back to the kitchen, and I went outside to play or maybe up to my room at the far end of the house. I don't remember saying a word.

It can't have been too long after that, though, that she stopped and pulled something out of her apron pocket and gave it to me. "It's a jaw harp," she said. When I didn't react, she stuck it in her mouth, and it and she began to make a strange, twangy sound.

She handed the strange thing to me, and it was cool and a little damp. It lay in my little-girl nightstand drawer for years. It never occurred to me to try. I felt nothing about it.

My mother, who is not interested in memory, tells me that Nora was about the same age as my grandmother. She had a son who was "not quite right," whom she supported by doing housework, going to a different house every day of the week. At some point, my mother says, Nora brought her the flag on one of her train trips to the suburbs. My mother supposes there was no place to display it in an apartment building.

The flag is a casket flag, given to Nora at the death of her husband, who was in the service in World War II. My mother does not think he died in the war, but she does not really know. It is big enough to have been laid on a coffin and covered it, to have been folded in that triangular fold and handed to the widow. It is muslin and well made and soft with age; the white stripes are cream-colored. The fabric on some stripes has worn quite away.

In the last stages of his illness-at-home, before he signed himself into a mental hospital and never came out, my father cut off all the household cash, including the ten dollars or so a week that had gone to Nora to keep those front rooms picked up. She was elderly by then and very stiff and slow. According to my mother, she didn't do much actual cleaning, although she still made chicken, as she had for fifteen years, every Thursday. In the front rooms of the big house, she polished the surfaces.

I doubt that Nora's separation from my family was done kindly or with any grace. Little was, in those days. My father shuffled around the house in his bathrobe, raging and then begging for pills. My older brother had gone off to college, safely away and distant. In high school then, I have no memory of a goodbye to Nora or of much else. I also do not remember the day of my father's commitment to the hospital, just a few weeks before I left for college and my own life, where I would trade in my lime-green matching pantsuit for wide-legged jeans worn ragged on the bottom and, for four years, watch protests go by but never join them.

Nora probably just got on the train one day for the last time and rode it back north into the city, disappearing into the life we'd never imagined. I doubt that anyone in our house gave it a thought.

I don't know when Nora died or how, or what became of her son. It was years before my hard-earned armor, pierced by the birth of my own children, permitted me to remember much about being the little girl with the braids at the piano or what happened over time in the big house with the backyard near the trains. In those years, I learned to sing, and forgot how, and remembered again. I continued to play piano as long as someone told me to, then stopped, and then began again. I worked in the musical theater, and it was that passionate work that finally taught me that music made me happy. I learned to listen and, at my best, I learned to let music wash through my heart and come back out again, carrying along pieces of my lost and forgotten feelings.

And I learned to open my eyes and see what was around me, women and men, friends and allies. I learned to see human connection, that synaptic splash of recognition and reciprocity, a kind of brief coupling and communion. It is a series of these splashes, these moments, these people, that illuminate our time as we travel from darkness to darkness.

I never thought of Nora during those years after she was

gone, but kindness does not go away forever. Even the smallest acts, like a moment at a piano or the gift of a jaw harp, reverberate in a child's deepest mind and are saved and remembered. Although I did not see them then, thirty-five years later, I recognize the gleam of joy in Nora's music and the touch of pity in her eye for the little girl and her music of piano parties and *plunk, plunk, plunk.* The bond is partly one of gender; after all this time, I recognize the warm woman's breeze of understanding. The mother in me now, remembering, thanks that old woman for her kindness to a little girl who was learning to play the piano without feeling a thing.

I like to think that Nora could tell that I had music inside me, carefully contained somewhere behind the new glasses and above the tight braids. She saw what I could not, being blank and blind to her, as I was blank and blind to so much outside and inside the doors of that difficult house.

On holidays now, my children and I go down to the basement and get out the old flag. They argue sometimes over who gets to fasten it to the rope with clips; Maggie's little hands are hardly big enough. "Eenie meenie minie mo," they say, choosing, "catch a tiger by the toe." My husband pulls the rope slowly. We hold hands and sing *The Star-Spangled Banner* as Nora's flag rises toward the blue sky over our farm. The kids sing the parts about the bombs bursting and the rockets; my husband hums along and smiles. And I throw my shoulders back and belt it out, standing with my family on the edge of the hill by the big pine tree in Minnesota. We have to start low at the beginning to be able to reach the high part at the end, and sometimes we just start over and over. Five hundred miles

and decades away from the past, we raise Nora's flag and
sing.

(1994, 2018)

Verse V

INCIDENTALS AND

PLEASURES

Miss Valentine at the Circus

The light is dim and uncertain. Beside the runway, on a flight of high steps, sits an old woman with a beautiful face and an amazing sequined hat. Beyond and all around, a sea of rapt faces stretches up and away, turned toward the central brilliance like a field of flowers. Scattered through the crowd are balloon men and ice cream men and men carrying poles dangling cones of cotton candy. The hawkers' hats have long black tassels and gold letters that spell, mysteriously, *Zuhrah*. Children in the audience wave light swords, à la *Star Wars*; many wear electric headbands that blink colors in the dark. There is an audible crunching in the air; the kids are eating as if they've just discovered food. Behind the bandstand, muscular men in exotic outfits are warming up with handsprings and cartwheels. One, a little older than the others, grins and waves at a little girl sitting sideways in her mother's lap. Mom is watching the ring; daughter is watching the acrobats. The girl lifts her hand solemnly, safe in the height of the bleachers. She says "hello" in a small voice and keeps eating.

Tethered to the wall are three brawny, honey-colored horses, a spotty-rumped Appaloosa, and a shaggy white pony with a painted circle around one eye. A handcart stands at the ready, heaped with a rainbow of sequined costumes. A big sombrero moves of its own accord. Turns out, there's a poodle underneath it. There are quite a few poodles back there animating clothes.

From above comes the blare of hard-driving band music with plenty of percussion and a hot first trumpet. The music ends with a flourish. The ringmaster calls boomingly

135

to the crowd, urging the children to let the performers know that an audience awaits. The response is piercingly treble, louder and louder as the ringmaster implores again and yet again. A lion coughs and speaks, and the roar is taken up by five other lions. Showgirls line up; small boys, and larger ones, too, whoop as they think they must. A moment's heady pause, and the showgirls plunge from the dark into the light. Framed by the bandstand, brilliant with color, filling three rings with Amazing Activity, Ferocious Felines, and Lovely Ladies; this is (yes!) the 66th Annual Zuhrah Shrine Circus.

Freeze it.

Take away light swords and battery-powered headbands. Move the scene, intact, from the 1980s Minneapolis Auditorium to 1908 and "the new armory building on Kenwood Boulevard." There the crowd was witnessing a brand-new phenomenon: an indoor circus. "In Europe," the *Minneapolis Journal* informed us, "the indoor circus is really the thing. . . . Arrangements for lighting the Armory brilliantly by electricity were made this week." The spectacle at hand was the Rhoda Royal Indoor Circus, "a travelling organization that has been appearing in a number of the large eastern cities." In fact, Rhoda Royal Indoor Circus had appeared just a few miles to the east in St. Paul, to a record-breaking attendance of forty thousand.

General admission cost fifty cents; reserved seats in the balcony cost an extra quarter, or two bits. Box seats were one dollar. Each day the papers published the names of the box seat purchasers for that evening's performance. One writer called the indoor circus "a more elaborate affair than the public understands or the Shriners themselves had counted on."

In 1908, the circus added a special attraction in the Cities: Oklahoma Bill's Cheyenne Frontier Wild West Show. Oklahoma Bill presided over "wild western sports" and, for the finale, the lynching of a horse thief. During Monday's opening-night opening number, a bucking bronco leaped the railing and tore into the crowd. The bronco-busting portion of the program was canceled. On Wednesday, a happy replacement was found: a free exhibition of bronco busting outside the Armory, on the Parade Grounds, 30 minutes before the main show. Fifty dollars was offered to anyone bold enough, brave enough, and skillful enough to ride High Tower, the bronco who had created such a sensation on opening night.

One wonders what the Shriners must have thought as High Tower vaulted the railing, scattering Minneapolitans like so many sparrows.

During the Circus Week of 1984, Shriners' red fezzes bobbed everywhere through the crowd at the Minneapolis Auditorium. Men's organizations can sometimes seem faintly sinister, with their lodges and funny hats and secret rites, but it was difficult to imagine a cheerier, more pleasant group of people than these Shriners. Each Shriner, whether selling peanuts or directing people to their seats, seemed to be having a genuinely good time; some took a Circus Week vacation every year and hadn't missed a performance in two decades.

In the dark confusion during *The Star-Spangled Banner*, I watched one Shriner escort a small child in the wake of a woman with a baby. The woman turned to him.

"Excuse me, but I think you have the wrong child," she said. "That one's not mine." The Shriner stopped, smiled, and herded his stray back in the direction from which they'd come. If he was groaning, it was inaudible.

The Shrine clowns, the Funsters, were much in evidence, having and making a good time. They warmed up the crowd, mingled with the kids, signed programs. They were also in the show in two elaborate routines featuring complicated props and dialogue with Colonel Lucky Larabee, ringmaster and straight man. The clowns talked to everybody. I saw a huddle group practicing to sign "hello" to deaf children. "They loved it! They just went nuts!" one Funster said later.

The sheer carefree fun of it all was justified, as if justification were needed, by the knowledge that the Shrine Circus was a fundraiser, a blood relative, if a distant one, of the bake sale. Shrine circuses from coast to coast support a network of Shrine hospitals and burn centers for children, where small patients can be treated free of charge. The Zuhrah Shriners estimated that Circus Week in Minneapolis would net something like $200,000 for kids in need—which just made the whole affair seem still more festive.

The frenzied pace of the Royal Hanneford Circus people puts "busy" to shame. Prop men, performers, and the producer dash from one task to the next, sometimes changing clothes en route. At the pre-circus press conference, a tall blonde woman said: "Well, I was hired as a clown, but then they found out I could sew, so I'm the wardrobe mistress now. I make half the wardrobe. And I'm a showgirl in the second half. I ride the elephants. I do production, too. I'll only be here 'til Wednesday, because then I have to go meet up with our second unit." With that, she rushed away to help with a birthday party.

Ina, one of the elephants, was turning fifteen. She had a cake. Her larger associate, Tina, helped her eat it. One of the elephant handlers, a thin man with glasses, anxiously questioned the Shriners and the publicity people: "There's no plastic or rubber in there? Nothing an elephant couldn't digest?"

During the show, the handler moved elephant props into and out of the ring at great speed, tapping insistently on one huge knee of a mammoth subordinate who relinquished a tub-top stance too slowly. Before and after each show, he supervised elephant rides (two dollars for twice around the ring—adults allowed, too), lifting children (mostly) into Tina's elaborate howdah and cautioning them to hold on. The girl helping the small elephant riders back down the steps was one of the equestriennes, minus spangles.

Few in the audience took notice of the restless metamorphoses all about them, as performers shed one spectacular skin in favor of another. It would have taken a keen eye to appreciate that the man who introduced the ringmaster in a red jacket and ruffles was also the man who appeared soon afterward, bare chested in tights, as the Artistic Aerial Astonishment, and who still later galloped past you in brilliant orange and feathers during the equestrian act, and who finally stood before you as an elephant handler. Your program listed this man as Superintendent of Properties.

On Wednesday, the wardrobe mistress/showgirl/clown went on to the second unit as promised, leaving a vacancy in the "Sequined and Spangled Spectacular: Journey With the Entire Cast of the Performers and Animals to a Childhood Land of Dreams and Experience Our All New Living Fairy Tale—Circus Holidays." The February holiday spot, Miss Valentine, stood empty.

Producer Tommy Hanneford, a resourceful fellow, saw me standing, taking notes, and smiling. He asked me if maybe I would like to go Out There. "Out There?" I said, stupidly. Hanneford gestured expansively toward the ring and, upon my astonished nod, collared a passing equilibrist. "Put her in the Valentine costume," he said, "and get her Out There."

"Come with me," said Miss Kim, "and hurry."

Miss Kim and I disappeared through some curtains behind the main hall, passing several quarreling children and a man from the Globe of Death at work on a motorcycle wheel. In the dressing room, long tables were covered with makeup and paraphernalia. Costume racks bulged with splendidly bright clothes—some so voluminous that they just barely fit on the hangers and others minimal, to say the least. If you have the body of an aerialist, you don't need much in the way of adornment. I was relieved to be handed a costume of the voluminous sort—entirely sequins and Velcro, with billowy sleeves and a hoop skirt spangled with hearts. It was red, quite decidedly red. Miss Kim, looking dubious, tossed me a sequined strip. "Do something with your hair," she said.

At the other end of the table, the lion tamer's wife was

changing clothes and telling about a time when the cats got away "and ran right up the aisles." (I had every reason to believe her, or at least to keep my mouth shut if I didn't. At the pre-circus press conference I'd attended, with cameras rolling, her husband had shouted "Sultan! Sultan!!" at one beast. The lion chose to remain seated until the tamer's wife ran around the outside of the cage and snapped: "Move it!" The lion moved it.)

A pretty woman with thick false eyelashes donned a pink cap to match the electric-pink leg wraps on her horse. "I think I will wear the pink today," she said and grinned. A young woman with a petulant face talked about her horse's work at the afternoon matinee. "God, he was a brat," she sighed.

I got out of my jeans and boots and into my costume. I struggled with my hair. "Does this happen often," I asked, "that some strange woman comes in here and gets into a costume?"

"All the time," she said.

An old woman, very old, came into the dressing room and began to change, slowly, into a long, gold-sequined gown. Then she put on a large, fuzzy, blue bathrobe. Mrs. Hanneford, the producer's mother, was ninety-five years old and traveling with the show. She came from "an old vaudeville family," and she looked wonderful in sequins.

Miss Kim, who had done a whole act while I was getting half ready, came back in for another change. She grabbed a red-and-white flower from a table. "Try putting that in your hair," she said and was gone.

A small boy walked up to me, now bedecked in red sequins and holding a notebook. He looked up. I waited. "Becky wears that costume," he said accusingly, then turned and walked away.

The time had come for my Sequined-and-Spangled circuit of the ring, and I took my place in line. I tried to strut. I managed to avoid falling over my hoop skirt, and there were no cries of "Fake!" or "Becky wears that costume!" If Colonel Larabee was astonished to see an unknown Miss Valentine parading toward him, he didn't show it. And the follow spots did not falter when they focused on me and my sequins. "Miss Valentine!" the colonel boomed, and I tried a pose. Then my moment was over.

The policemen backstage, also Shriners, rewarded my performance with grins and hugs. "We've been working this show for years," one said, "and we've never gotten Out There." They went looking for a camera. I said that I felt fortunate that none was handy. But no one (not even I) believed it. I was a little slow getting back into my jeans.

The circus has a backstage as well as its show-off side. It is close and purposeful behind the bandstand. Everyone knows precisely what needs to be done. It's like an actor's green room, where energy seems half suspended. While the Funsters are Out There exploding an outhouse that turns out to be a phone booth, the equestrian act is starting to assemble—the riders in orange and sequins. The women carry spears with feathers drooping down and lean them against the bandstand while making last-minute adjustments to their hair and body stockings. They are lithe and strong-looking, with makeup heavy enough to withstand the ring's

142

intense lights. The horse trainer (who is also the elephant trainer) is in a blue, skin-tight, and faintly iridescent costume. His fancy jacket conceals a secret stash of carrots.

The big horses are held by the bridles before going out, but they don't seem impatient. The pony walks loose, responding to a low whistle when he roams too far. He practices his tricks in the dark for a carrot reward. Walking behind his trainer, the pony scoots unexpectedly between his legs. The riders laugh a little. As the music changes, they move toward the runway and grab their spears. Hanneford takes up a whip from the prop table and moves out with them. He will handle the horses, as his family has handled them for several generations, while the riders leap and somersault. One of the prop men whispers to me that the big, gray Percheron was a farm horse. When the circus people first saw him, he was pulling a plow. The farm horse trots by, steady and massive, going to work. Hurricane Hoof Beats takes the center ring.

Public attention is a hard thing to get these days, and it has never been an easy proposition to bring a single cry of surprise or applause from six thousand people. But in a world increasingly populated with lunatic media thrills— where the flick of a switch can bring you anything from multiple car crashes to the Battle of the Network Stars, all in full color—the circus is a comforting place, home to the fantastic but not to fantasy. The circus is unswervingly real, unmistakably not television. There is real danger and real spectacle in every act. Spectators are properly awed, properly alarmed. And if the aura of excitement dissipates fifteen or twenty rows back, well, buy your seats farther down, ringside, close enough to smell the lions and see the sweat on the aerialists. Buy popcorn. Applaud wildly. Then savor the moment when all danger is past, when the performers return in their capes and costumes for the Fantastic Flag-Waving Finale.

Mrs. Hanneford, blue robe discarded, is escorted to the center ring like a queen. The follow spots strike fire from her gold sequins. When the ringmaster introduces her, she smiles brilliantly and casts off fifty years. Flags fall from the rigging over all three rings. The ringmaster takes off his hat. The band pauses. In the audience, a Zuhrah clown lifts a child high to see the moment. "God bless America!" Colonel Larabee cries, "And Mrs. Hanneford!"

(1984)

How to Watch High School Basketball

High school basketball is a long, long season. Even for the most rabid fans or family members, four months is a long time to spend sitting twice a week in a succession of high school gyms, blinking under the fluorescents and flanked by strangers shouting imprecations against your offspring. For those to whom its rules and rituals are a mystery, there comes a time along about week six or seven when the mind cries out for more. We have no desire to master the arcane details; we'll never understand, or care, what the passionate cry "box out!" means. We just want something to watch. Here are a few suggestions to carry us through.

Take basketball shoes. Disregarding the fact that we are going to the poorhouse from buying them, try now to appreciate their finer qualities. Become a connoisseur. Admire their curves, their colors, their strange alien conformation, their simple hugeness. Are there actual human feet in there? Whatever happened to white socks, or any socks?

While considering style, watch the players repeatedly, unthinkingly, pull their hugely baggy shorts down over their hips while coming down the court and even on the free throw line. Elastic is pulling toward the actual waistline; fashion requires those shorts to go south. Which force will triumph?

Ponder the place of cheerleading in the modern world. This is a rich vein of inquiry, even if you skip right over the question of the outfits. Or watch the coaches. Contemplate the imminence of coronaries. What is the best path for emergency medical personnel to enter the gym?

Institute a private study of fan behavior. Self-select for the positive ones. Put aside the sullen, the resentful, the know-it-alls. If necessary, move away from your husband or partner. Concentrate on the stalwart, the enthusiastic, the intent, and the hopeful. Try to guess which parents belong with which player. Eavesdrop all you like.

Assign yourself a personal scoring system. Five points if you can figure out who the captains are without reading the program. Ten points for spotting any player trying to grow facial hair. A fifty-point bonus for catching a glance from the court, with or without grin, between a player and his parents.

But here's the best way to really watch high school basketball. Forget trying to follow the ball; that's what everybody else is doing. To really understand the game, pick one player and watch only him. Choose a kid with an interesting face or an interesting hairdo or an interesting attitude. Watch him on the bench and while he crouches at the side, waiting to come into the game. Watch him with the ball in his hands and after it leaves him. You will be amazed.

The boys move like dancers, like gazelles, albeit very large gazelles. They throw the ball violently to an empty place, which then is suddenly filled with a teammate's hands. They swirl, they circle, they dash furiously from place to place without apparent purpose, until a purpose suddenly appears. They clomp, they leap, they screech to a halt. They look everywhere at once. They switch hands without effort. They bounce the ball through their legs and behind their backs. They handle it without ever looking at it.

They know what they are doing, even if you don't.

Let others opine about "the press" and "the posts" and mutter continually, "why doesn't he put him in?" Choose your one player, any player, and watch. No matter what is on the scoreboard, you will be in the personal contentment zone. In the player, you see effort, dedication, athleticism, and emotions ranging from determination to frustration to exhilaration. You may never figure out what "over and back" is, but you'll still understand the sport.

Our season is getting toward playoffs, and I've lost track of the win-loss ratio. Last game, against a school that beat us by thirty points last season, I saw a player knocked to the floor so hard his head bounced. One of his teammates half-carried him to the bench while another sent for ice. Then they looked at each other, went back into the game, and came within five points of winning. There might have been some boxing out involved, or maybe some over-and-backing. I really have no idea.

But I was watching those boy faces as they helped their teammate off the floor and then came back on. And I get the game; I absolutely get it. It's really something to watch.

(2003)

The Klingons Play Ball—For Forty Years

It wasn't the Twins, so it must have been the Kleons who taught me to look at baseball. The name was supposed to be *Klingons*, but when the team was phone-registered in the University of Minnesota Softball League in 1971, somebody couldn't spell. Instead of being a race of aggressive alien space warriors, à la *Star Trek*, it became the "Kleons," and that obscurity only affirmed my affable disinterest when I married onto the team. If I'd realized they were really Klingons . . . well, who knows?

But softball? Why would you? Early-period field hockey in high school had not inspired me to a life of team sport, and nothing about major league sports ever changed my mind.

The seasons rolled by. I got to know them, and discovered that the Kleons were interesting, though in a backward kind of way. Instead of watching the ball or the bat or the score, I started watching the players. There's a Rick, a Jack, an Ed, a Jerry. They are undemonstrative regular guys, including a banker, a contractor, and a couple of small-business owners. It was intriguing to see how they loved to play, rushed to the field after long workdays, and lingered over a beer and a bag of corn chips as the sun's light got low after a game, hitting a few balls out to their children. It was interesting how, every year, somebody came up with a new design for the team shirt and new affectionate jokes and awards for the team dinner.

I watched them for a couple of years before I realized how beautiful they were. By then they were all pushing forty, and not a matinee idol among them, including my own good

149

husband. But they had the unselfconscious grace of absolute focus, moving like one creature on and off the field. Concentrating and playing hard, they were filled with energy and attention, hope and cunning, facing some younger team with slimmer middles and more fashionable hair. Something in the game made them beautiful.

I started to pay more attention. I picked up some of Roger Angell's elegant prose for my husband and read it myself, skipping the numbers but lingering over the infused rhythm of the game. There was the real-guy smile of Kirby Puckett and his rock solidness in the Annie Leibovitz photograph on the cover of a local magazine. And in the Ken Burns documentary on baseball history, I was struck by the rich, reflective tone of the voice-over and the pure glee of men like Robert Creamer, talking about how they just plain love the game.

And in due course, I participated in the utter hilarity of kindergarten T-ball, where balls roll by unheeded while shoes are tied and parent assistants spring from the field with little players in tow, aiming desperately for the nearest bathroom. In the first-grade level, a team we played had a child in a wheelchair, who was brought, grinning, up to the "T." When he tapped off the ball, his teammates rushed to the plate and pushed him, careening and screaming, around the bases. Major league baseball just never looked like that much fun.

We found some of that fun at St. Paul Saints games at the old Municipal Stadium, although we were never there when the weather was good. We were either huddled under umbrellas or draped in blankets. But even against a chill wind blowing up the bleachers, you could see what the Kleons feel and what child players thrill to. The game is beautiful. It has pace and rhythm and drama and ambition. It has tension and humor. In the old stadium, and in the shiny new Saints ballpark, it has immediacy.

We even buy teamwear, although licensed sportswear products are mostly annoying; desire for a T-shirt seems based on what team has the most pugnacious graphics. But my little son wore his Saints hat to school every day, under his stocking cap with the long tail. He knew the Saints and the Kleons were his teams. He and his little sister wore their father's old team shirts for pajamas and sick days. And now, my workout hoodie says *Saints* across the front.

Over the years, the aliens grayed and added some elaborate knee braces to their gear, but the Kleons still played tough slow-pitch in an open league where other teams might be half their age and have twice their speed. Some thirty years after they started, manager Jack Griffin said, often, "My usual starting lineup *averages* age forty-nine or so. But, like Waylon, we believe that age and treachery beat out youth and skill every time." Every year they tried to prove it, out on the fields of Arden Hills. And every year, the Nakers tried to prove them wrong.

The Nakers, obscurely named from a long-ago game of Balderdash, are the team that formed around the Kleon sons, who all started playing ball with their dads in postgame playtime when they were too small to throw as far as the pitcher's mound. They grew up wanting to be Kleons and then turned into players who wanted to, in a filial kind of way, whip 'em.

After they were first matched up, it took eight long years and sixteen games for the Nakers to beat the Kleons. The overall record stands at twenty-seven wins for the old guys and eight for the young ones. Every game was friendly, close-fought, and hard-nosed and then dissected over a case of beer. In 2007 and '08, the Nakers swept the Klingons over five games, but in the last two seasons they played each other, the Kleons came back to beat them four times. The Nakers won none. Jack the manager still laughs about it: "At the end, they got freaked out and so tense that they just couldn't play!"

Postgame barbecues matter, and beer matters. There was a year when the Kleons won the league (2004, eleven and two, and they beat the Nakers twice); they celebrated by commissioning special labels for beer bottles and then applied them to a case or two of Killian's Red. After the last game, they broke out the Kleons beer and drank it in the parking lot. "Ah," they said. "That championship beer is smooth."

A small-business owner, my husband, sponsored the team for thirty-two of its forty years. We have a large stock of hats in the closet and a full set of jerseys. The Kleons favored fancy shirts and slogans, always printed in Klingon, a language whose alphabet is mostly triangles, and sometimes printed upside down so players could glance down if they need inspiration. (Who could tell?) The slogans evolved from truculence toward the rueful, and were largely dreamed up, as they say, "after a couple of beers." They reflect the passage of time and were the source of some confusion for opponent teams.

"Weapons of past destruction," the shirts said one year. "Do you really want to take on 817 years of experience?" And "Get to know them before they forget who they are." "Wider is better," the shirts said one year and, in another, in honor of their aging knees, "Snap, crackle, pop."

The slogan in 1998, one year after the sons started their eight-year losing streak with their fathers, was "Not this year, Nakers." It must have taken considerable analysis to figure out how to write "Nakers" in Klingon.

It was never really good for the Kleons when there was a Minnesota cold snap during softball season. Better that the ambient temperature should at least be higher than the age of the founding members. Or else they can't bend. I remember one year when the veteran softball team, closing their thirty-fourth season together, entered the Arden Hills Men's Upper Division playoff series at 7 PM on a Tuesday night in August, in a rising wind with a record-breaking air temperature of fifty-five degrees. The founding members were fifty-five, fifty-six, and fifty-seven. One or two of them layered a long-sleeved shirt under their uniform. A few stretched to limber up before they strapped on their various knee and elbow braces. Then they settled their hats, stepped out, and took the field. They were league and playoff champions that year.

The Kleon trophy collection is held in the manager's garage and various player basements. They played hard and efficiently, and they won. Over forty years of play, they held seventeen championships; their heyday was in the eighties and nineties, with twelve trophies. In 1986, they entered a

Division I tournament and swept it with six victories. "That was our shining hour," they say; I wonder how you say that in Klingon.

There are plenty of glittering athletes in the world. I am sure their skills are remarkable, their dedication intense, their focus complete. The Kleons, and all their humble hometown ilk, demonstrate another side. Playing together for forty years, for the pleasure and the competition and the companionship and the testosterone of it, is one way of loving sports and one way of living a life based on athletic principles. Play hard, every time. Be *on* the team. Come back next year.

I remain an irritating companion for true-believer fans. I'm not interested in statistics, and I am liable to be distracted from play by such nonessentials as wondering what they're actually saying to each other out there on the mound. At Saints games, I often could not tell you who the opposing team was or name a single player. But my family watched the players scowl and scramble, had our faces painted, and always laughed long over that shark race, imagining some poor Saints staffers running around the outside of the fence, holding up wooden fish on sticks. In the old stadium looking up beyond the diamond, we saw the lights of the state fair Midway spinning and twirling. The fire department was working out on its practice building right next door. A freight train rumbled by, hooting. In the new stadium, dusk is generally falling as the game begins. Actors roam the seats making children smile; you can get a haircut back above the outfield. The team mascot wears a pig costume with a short skirt and is called Mudonna. There is also a live pig who carries balls out to the ump; every year two thousand people enter a contest to name it (Notorious P.I.G.; Little Red Porkette). Our seats are along the third base line; I can see the pitcher look around for his checks. Then he settles and looks hard at the batter, who also quiets. There is a moment of suspension, and then a powerful unwinding to the pitch. After that, anything can happen.

This year, I'm not very interested in what's going to happen with the Twins, or with any major league sports. The professionals are not my culture; the skills displayed do not outweigh the baggage.

But I do thank you, Mr. Veeck and Mr. Murray, for the Saints. Mr. Puckett. Mr. Burns. All members of the Withrow T-ball teams. And thank you, Kleons. I couldn't see it before; it has come on very slowly. But now, I'm looking forward to the season.

(2010)

Riding in the *Bootle-Bumtrinket*

Some of us spend a considerable amount of time looking for funny books to read. Definitions vary, of course—*The Pickwick Papers* is not to everyone's taste, and neither is *Bossypants*—and any kind of humor can be in short supply in our tumultuous lives, full of daily barrages of information and jam-packed calendars posted on refrigerator doors and crowding up our smartphones. That's why people read the funnies, still love Dave Barry and Molly Ivins, repeat jokes at the office, and share those clever memes.

Humor comes in categories; mean jokes are easy jokes, based on fear. (See, I'm laughing: I'm one of you! Don't turn on me!) Happy humor meant for adults is more difficult to make. Those who are gifted with the ability to see the good-hearted humor in the bigger world are rare and precious. It's a small cohort who can appreciate the world's complexities and joys, its resilience and its good strong heart, and communicate these pleasures. Their work, largely, is not subject to the passage of time.

I saw in our local paper that one of those rare ones had died. I don't normally read the obituaries, but I stopped when I saw, under Deaths Elsewhere, in bigger type, "Gerald Durrell, Naturalist, Author" and thought about it a bit. Gerald Durrell, at least once, wrote a truly wonderful book. That's what the headline should have said.

Durrell was one of those whose humor and invention are durable. Neither the passage of years nor his death diminishes the pleasure of reading his work. *My Family and Other Animals* was first published in 1956, the year I turned six. It is set on the island of Corfu in the mid-1930s, when my mother was in her teens. I first read it when my children were small, and I have just given it to my daughter-in-law.

I knew at once I was in for a treat when I read, in an introductory section called "The Speech for the Defence," that the book "was originally intended to be a mildly nostalgic account of the history of the island, but I made a grave mistake by introducing my family into the book in the first few pages." He continues: "Having got themselves on paper, they then proceeded to establish themselves and invite various friends to share the chapters. It was only with the greatest difficulty, and by exercising considerable cunning, that I managed to retain a few pages here and there which I could devote exclusively to animals."

It's a wonderful voice, an adult who still possesses a clear-seeing ten-year-old's view of the world, a resoundingly curious boy who plunges happily into a world filled with incident and natural mystery and who, accompanied by three dog companions, Roger, Widdle, and Puke, has the run of the island and the culture. His world is filled with eccentric and loving humans, loyal animal pets, and fascination with the tremendous mysteries of the natural world. Young Gerry looks at the activities of dung beetles with passionate attention and reports the doings of his family in a straightforward reportorial style, even when they are most ridiculous. Brother Larry, then twenty-three, who turned out later to be the novelist Lawrence Durrell, is present in this story as a short-statured and acerbic big brother, who first suggests that his family move out of the raw English climate to the Greek islands. It is an impulse with which writers from Minnesota will easily identify. "I can't be expected to produce deathless prose," he says, "in an atmosphere of gloom and eucalyptus."

Their arrival in Corfu is complicated by a tremendous assortment of bags, a "magnificently dilapidated horse-drawn cab," and their large dog Roger, who did not want to get in: "Eventually we had to lift him bodily and hurl him inside, helping frantically, and then pile in breathless after him and hold him down. The horse, frightened by this activity, broke into a shambling trot, and we ended in a tangled heap on the floor of the cab with Roger moaning loudly underneath us. 'What an entry,' said Larry bitterly. 'I had hoped to give an impression of gracious majesty, and this is what happens. We arrive in town like a troupe of medieval tumblers.'"

The section following this, when the cab is pursued to the hotel by an indignant yapping herd of dogs, provoked howls of laughter from my very modern children, some thirty years after the words were written and ninety years after the events took place. I await the howls of my daughter-in-law.

"Living in Corfu was rather like living in one of the more flamboyant and slapstick comic operas," Durrell remembered. Through young Gerry's eyes, the island is soaked in sun, covered from one end to the other with fascinating creatures, and filled with scientific clues that yield every day to the observant eye and a boy's collecting kit. The book is affectionate, sentimental, and funny, and it rides on appreciation of the natural world in the same way that Gerald Durrell's homemade boat, the *Bootle-Bumtrinket*, rode on the surface of the blue sea.

From reading the little biographical page at the front of my paperback edition and the even smaller obituary in the newspaper, I see that Durrell, a complete stranger to me outside this one volume, actually did many other things in his life. He "collected" animals all over the world. He made expeditions to places I have never heard of. He made television programs and founded a zoological park. He wrote, this material tells me, thirty-seven books, and they have been translated into thirty-one languages.

The bit about the thirty-seven books is wonderful news in our family. The local bookseller reports that they have only one title in stock, but the library has many more. I particularly like the sound of one called *The Amateur Naturalist*; it was followed one year later by *How to Shoot an Amateur Naturalist*. And, most happy discovery, two of them are companion volumes to *My Family and Other Animals*. I'll be able to go back to Corfu this spring, for more rambles around the island with Gerry and Roger. Paddling through a warm Mediterranean bay with a collecting bag sounds like something very close to heaven.

Durrell is gone. However, one full ocean and half a continent away, years after his death and nearly a century after he was a boy, a family of strangers is reading his work, learning a little about the natural world, and laughing out loud. It is a small thing and a happy legacy. I have the feeling that Durrell might have appreciated it. We certainly do.

(1995)

The Wreck of *The Equator*

Watching the St. Croix River come out of its winter sleep is one of the many pleasures of spring in the east metro, and folks who live close by the water sometimes watch to see which is the first boat to venture out.

But back in the day, the St. Croix was a working river, the easiest and sometimes the only way to get between settlements and towns. And in April, after the long, long winter, people were more than ready to get out of town.

One morning in April of 1858, a stern-wheel steamboat called *The Equator* pulled out of Prescott, Wisconsin, crowded with three hundred "excursionists" headed upriver on the St. Croix for Stillwater. The river ice had opened early that season, and the winter-weary passengers were off to hear a travel lecture. The wind was strong and out of the north. They did not arrive.

This tale survives in a first-person story told by the "cub" pilot, the young-and-learning pilot, who was on *The Equator* that day. It was first published in 1909 in the flowery language of the day, but the hard winds and sudden weather changes are familiar to all who know the river, which is in places more than a mile from shore to shore. When *The Equator* passed Catfish Bar heading north and the river opened up wide and clear, the same way it does today, "the sweep of the wind raised a great sea and the heavily-laden boat crawled ahead into the teeth of the blizzard, for it began to snow as well as blow." They were three miles above Afton, in the widest part of the river, when one of the engines threw a rod and the paddlewheel stopped.

"As soon as the wheel stopped," Captain Merrick recalled,

> the boat fell off into the trough of the sea. The first
> surge caught her on the quarter, before she had
> fully exposed her broadside, but it rolled her lee
> guards under water, and made every joint in her
> upper works creak and groan. The second wave
> struck her full broadside on. As the boat rolled
> down, the tables, which had just been set for
> dinner, were thrown to leeward with a crash of
> broken glass and china. Women and children
> screamed; men turned white and some began to
> scramble and fight for life preservers . . . many
> deck hands dropped to their knees, making strong
> vows of religious reformation should they come
> safe to land, two miles away.

It took fifteen minutes, with the waves sweeping over the
lower deck and water pouring into the hold, for the mate to
rouse those devout deckhands to drop the spars, lash
together a sea anchor, and throw it overboard to steady *The
Equator*:

> In the ten or fifteen minutes that it had taken to get
> the drag built and overboard, the waves had swept
> over the lower deck and into the hold, until there
> was a foot of water weighing her down, which the
> bilge pumps were unable to throw out as fast as it
> came in. Had it continued to gain for fifteen
> minutes longer, the boat would have gone to the
> bottom with all on board. The drag saved the
> vessel; the coolness and quickness of the mate and
> carpenter were the salvation of the steamer and its

great load of people.

And then the steamboat drifted, driven by the storm, until it struck the shore on the Wisconsin side just above Afton, where it quickly broke up. "The men carried the women ashore through four feet of water. Big fires were built from the wreckage to warm the wet and benumbed people. Runners were sent to nearby farmhouses for teams. Many of the men walked home to Prescott and Hastings." The "bones," the wreckage of the boat, were still visible broadside to the beach as late as 1909.

And that was how that happy April boating excursion ended on our very own St. Croix River, 153 years ago this month. Watch the weather on the river this spring, as you drive along its banks or cross it on wide bridges. There will likely be a snowstorm or two; and if you look closely, you might glimpse through the snow *The Equator*, in peril and coming safe to shore with not one life lost.

(2016)

Wooden Horses

A two-line ad in the classifieds of the *Minneapolis Star Tribune*, antiques section, decades ago, led me into one of the earliest of my collecting passions. "Carousel horses. Serious inquiries only," it said, and a phone number from the western suburbs. When I called, I had to present my bona fides. Who was I? What was my interest? And, tellingly, after a pause, "Tell me," she said. "You sound young. Do you have a thousand dollars?"

I remember the day I drove out in my little car, following general directions through the prosperous suburbs, into the wealthy exurb, toward the shores of the secluded and exclusive lake. There was a gate and a gatehouse, unstaffed, and a long curving drive through mature trees, with a glint of water in the distance. I parked in the circle, stepped up to the massive front door. When it opened, I caught a glimpse of a foyer with a curving staircase and a full-length formal portrait of a young be-gowned woman. It was my hostess, who now was no longer young and without the gown. She quickly vetted my clothes and manner. "They're in the stables," she said and led the way.

It was late afternoon in the fall, and a slanting golden light was coming through the trees and touching everything. The stables were long and low. No horses were in evidence. She led me in through the end, into a dusty runway with box stalls on both sides. The stalls had Dutch doors, closed; she walked ahead, opening the top halves on the western side, and that golden light spilled through the frames, poured in, making bright squares and picking up the motes of hay we stirred as we walked. In three or four of the boxes were tall piles of wooden carousel horses, not stacked or racked, but jumbled one on the other. Here a prancing leg protruded, there an arched neck or a face with a lively eye and flaring nostrils. They appeared to be rearing or running. They were simultaneously active and frozen. They were all white, everywhere.

I brought one home, of course, after a long, pleasant time of looking and considering. I was aware that I was infused with something new. It was the beginning of ten or fifteen years of intense interest in and activity surrounding vintage carousel pieces. Oh, I scouted and searched. I bought and sold. Each piece has a provenance and also an origin story.

I own a German horse, also white, with a powerful prancing body and two missing hind legs, discovered by chance in the window of a T-shirt shop in NYC, stapled all over with "sale today" signs. I walked in and cut a happy deal; the owner surely thought he was taking me for a ride, and I knew I was taking him for a ride. I offered him more money if he could find the missing legs, but no. I picked it up in a station wagon hired from the back pages of the old *Village Voice*. I wrapped that horse in packing blankets and stuffed it into the tied-down trunk of a one-way-drive vehicle and drove back to the Midwest in the same time period that everyone in America was looking for Jimmy Hoffa's body. We were not stopped.

I own an old fellow with tin ears, fixed up with Bondo, found in the backyard grass of a barn in Michigan. I own a carousel goat from a small-town auction where I was the only bidder until they realized I was interested; a staffer bid me up, but it was still a bargain. (Bring the pickup truck, I

166

messaged my husband. I've bought a goat.) A friend was once riding his bike by the display window of a furniture store across town and spotted a horse. I bought it, a beautiful shape like an oversize weather vane, with terribly deteriorated legs; once it had stood out in the snow year-round with a shop sign. I own one horse in its original paint, seen in blurry photographs from the early twentieth century, when the ride cost five cents. And I have a rare Indian pony, carved with a warrior head and a lariat.

For years, I made a round of biannual phone calls to all the antique dealers in the region. One said he had something and met me at his mother's house in St. Paul. I followed him through a tuck-under garage into the basement, where damp laundry was hanging from one end to the other. We parted the clothes with our hands. An enormous wood carving was leaning against the far wall. From a British roundabout, circa 1890, deeply gilded with flags and a portrait of a general from the Boer War. I can see it from where I sit at my desk.

I bought books and studied them. I subscribed to newsletters and went to conventions (yes, there were conventions). And when the famous and beloved Minnesota State Fair carousel came into jeopardy, to be sent to a New York auction house to be broken up, I joined the effort to save it, chairing the restoration committee for a time. I dove into the dusty fair scrapbooks first and then expanded my research, pleasantly wandering in old times and places and practices.

The excerpt below is from an unpublished history of that carousel, Philadelphia Toboggan Company #33.

The sun shines particularly brightly around a carousel in the morning. Perhaps it's because the usual accompaniments of colored bulbs are missing, letting natural light pick out an upraised ear here or a curving foreleg there. There is no inviting crash of music; sometimes a breeze or a birdsong can be heard, or the sound of a broom or the tread of a workman whose solitary weight shifts the round platform, hanging from its center pole. There is no movement, no fool-the-eye illusion of speed and energy, no flash of mirrors. The horses are still when they're off duty; a careful eye can see the marks of years of scuffing and wear where children's knees have gripped and little hands have flailed the reins against the wooden necks. Dust moves in the shafts of light, and it is quiet in the same way that a theater is quiet when it is empty. Last night, the space was filled with people and movement and noise. There was exuberance and the boundless energy of children. These things leave their traces. A careful ear, standing quietly in the morning by a stationary carousel, can hear them.

Philadelphia Toboggan Company Carousel #33, brought to Minnesota in 1914 and still carrying riders, speaks to the attentive observer about things that don't change over time, and things that do. Over the decades, the first person to come in in the morning might have arrived by foot or streetcar, by bus or car. They might have worn rough boots and a workman's cap or overalls, or later, when they also might be female, they might be in sweats and tennies. The workers might be called casual labor, or help, or, later, volunteers.

Still, the morning examination of the machine is much the same. Walk around it, slowly. Loose cables? Loose legs? Test the music—the band organ or the Wurlitzer. A brief blare before the quiet returns. Flip the lights on and walk around again; replace burned-out bulbs so the electrical outlines of spokes and circles will be perfect. Then, two sharp hits on the fog bell as a warning, and push the button or throw the long-handled clutch.

Without the covering music, the carousel whines as it begins and the sound moves up in register as speed increases. The horses begin to rise and fall, all sixty-eight carved bodies in a forest of dizzy movement. The worker walks around the carousel as it spins, glancing at all the various joints and braces, moving as one would on the deck of a heaving ship, lightly balancing a hand on a horse's rising rump or falling saddle. The carousel goes very fast when it is empty of people, and if there are early spectators, they always gasp when the worker swings up to the wooden framework above the horses. Up there, one has to hold on tight, and watch everything move, and listen for any undue creaks or new rubbing or groaning sounds that might indicate a problem. Check the lubrication. There must be enough for smooth operation of all those moving parts, but not so much as to drip on the patrons, please.

These things do not change.

On the ground, ticket takers and cashiers arrive. In the early days, regardless of the weather, they were professionally dressed, the men in suits and ties and the women in skirts, white high-necked blouses, and hair tucked up and away behind. Later, skirts rose, legs appeared, and men took off their jackets and sometimes their hats. These people were often members of the family that owned the carousel at any given time; they thought of the carousel time as a kind of family reunion. Later, the formal clothing gave way to the ubiquitous jeans and sneakers on college kids hired to help out. Later still, volunteers came, casually dressed but with the same attention to a child looking up at the dangling stirrup of a large horse. Rolls of tickets are a constant, although the price has risen over the years. There was always a ticket booth; there was always a cashbox. These are the things that make the carousel possible.

In the world outside, nothing seemed to remain the same. The wooden carousel with its horses and chariots, music and lights has stood through two world wars and the Great Depression and persisted through many smaller conflicts and economic tides long after the fashion of naming them so grandly was over. When it began its long life of turning and pleasure, Woodrow Wilson was president and *Tarzan of the Apes* was a new novel. Since then, most families have turned over three complete generations, perhaps four. Many of them have marked the years by annual rides on the old carousel.

In the beginning, the light reached for the carousel and its painted horses through the cracks and open doors of a dusty building on the fairgrounds; these days, it is surrounded by glass doors that can be flung open to the summer weather. But still: since 1914, the morning light in Minnesota has appeared and disappeared and found the carousel the same, filled with the enormous static charge of the joy of children, ready to turn again.

In 1914, one Austin McFadden, then of Grand Rapids, Michigan, contracted with the Minnesota State Agricultural Society for the construction and erection of a giant roller coaster and a giant merry-go-round on the grounds of the Minnesota State Fair.

McFadden was in the middle of a long and prosperous career in the burgeoning amusement park industry. Before the invention of television and the proliferation of radio, before the world became hectic, before leisure meant an afternoon with a video screen, the families of America were learning what Europeans had known for much longer. On a Sunday afternoon, on a day of rest, it was a pleasant occupation to journey to a place made only for amusement, a little removed from the normal round of work and home and far removed in spirit from the weekday. Parks and green spaces were soothing; picnics were refreshing; boat rides were relaxing. Embellishments on the theme of soothing, refreshing, and relaxing were even better. A park that included attractions and rides could be cool and shady in one place and decorously riotous in another. Dancing was a pleasure in a pavilion with a good floor and a good orchestra. Young women could proceed from a gracefully laid-out picnic and moments later be leaning on their escort's arm as the floor shifted in a funhouse; children could leave their games and hop on a merry-go-round to bravely spear the ring for a free ride.

Since the 1903 opening of Luna Park in Coney Island, with its elaborate rides and attractions, a wave of development of amusement areas had crossed the country. In Minnesota,

Big Island Park in Lake Minnetonka was reached by excursion boat. Later, the east side of St. Paul would favor Wildwood, with city families riding to the very end of the trolley line, then boarding a boat to cross White Bear Lake to the park. Both parks, of course, had merry-go-rounds, a staple for operators interested in attracting families to their amusement locations.

McFadden's work in the amusement industry carried him repeatedly from coast to coast in a time when most people's lives were lived out in a small geographical circle of community and town. A likable, shrewd man, he knew people and what they liked. He was a consummate promoter; his other ventures included a traveling dancing school that moved from town to town in the Midwest, teaching locals the latest steps from the coast. McFadden himself, tuxedoed, was the main instructor. He also conducted a traveling tent exhibition of an early airplane, displayed on a sawdust floor. When the fascinated crowd moved too slowly for McFadden, he would turn on the engine and blow his coughing customers out the flaps, making room for the next set of nickels. But in 1914, his place of business was the Minnesota State Fair, a much larger kind of amusement venue.

Begun as a kind of boosterism for Minnesota's agricultural industry and as a form of mutual support in a state where the weather can only be described as non-supportive, the fair had already been through several stages of development and several good solid Minnesota arguments by 1914. After being held in various locations around the state for years "with little measure of success" and being sought by business interests in both the rival cities of Minneapolis and

St. Paul, it had settled on grounds midway between the two cities in 1885, after a "secret maneuver" by the capital city granted two hundred acres of the Ramsey County Poor Farm, free of charge, to the fair.

By 1914, the Minnesota State Fair was hugely successful and heavily attended, shining with the improvements of years of solid support and enthusiasm. It had enormous permanent buildings, including a grandstand that seated twelve thousand, and was connected directly to the city waterworks. A new crosstown streetcar line on Snelling Avenue had been built. There was a freight terminal, an emergency hospital, and gas service, thereby eliminating "the ragged assortment of gasoline stoves which has always been a menace." In 1910, secretary C. N. Cosgrove reported, "It is a commonly accepted fact that the Minnesota State Fair is doing as much or more, annually, to advertise the great State of Minnesota, and at the same time to educate its citizens as to the resources of the State and how to get the most out of them, than any other institution in the State. I need not inform you that the attendance of the Fair is nearly double that of any other Fair in the United States."

But the streets were all dirt, and sidewalks were nonexistent. Electric lights had only arrived at the fair a few years earlier and were still a novelty to many of the farm folk who came to the Cities for the big event. The fair lasted six days then. Its timing had been the cause of much argument over the years, with farmers from the northern part of Minnesota concerned that a pre–Labor Day fair did not allow sufficient maturation of their crops to make them competitive with the comparatively balmy counties from

173

the southwest part of the state. Competitive agricultural displays were a major focus of the fair in those days, with towering buildings made of apples and potatoes, marvelously detailed frescoes of corn and wheat sheaves, proudly and laboriously designed and constructed by county representatives. The building that housed them was rated as the largest agricultural exposition building in the world. The stock barns were also the focus of much pride and labor. New strains of livestock and methods of increasing productivity in beef and dairy products were much discussed, and competitors washed and brushed and combed their animals and themselves for that culminating moment in the show ring. Agricultural technology was changing fast enough and information transmission was still limited enough that the fair was a vital time of exchange of new ideas and methods. As early as 1902, "educational authorities held that there is more to be learned in a single day at the State Fair than in double the time in school or college." The fair's pressmen reported that the school boards in Minneapolis and St. Paul set back the opening day of school until Monday after the fair.

This is not to say that there was no frivolity. Even in the earliest days the amusement side of the fair, although less touted, was both heavily publicized and patronized. "By 1896 the Minnesota State Fair had a Sixty-foot Ferris wheel. By 1897, there was a full-fledged state fair Midway, with merry-go-round, a fortune-teller, a 'grinning Ethiopian' who stuck his head through a piece of canvas and dared comers to hit him with a ball, a strong man, a fat lady, and an illusion that permitted a look at the insides of a genuine, transparent 'x-ray woman.'" Hot dogs, popcorn, and lemonade of a violent pink hue were sold throughout. In 1904, the shows and rides that had been scattered all over the grounds were put into a new enclosure called "The Merry Pike." The Pike carnival contract went to various presenters over the years; independent attractions were also on the grounds, on a percentage basis. In 1913, there were nineteen of those shows and amusements, including two merry-go-rounds, a Ferris wheel, a flea circus, and a Miniature of a Model Mine.

These two reigning activities of the fair were not always in harmony. From its early days, there were annual calls for concentration on the serious business of agriculture and an annual decrying of the amusement side. Some people, vocal people, seemed to feel that "going over the Pike," as it was sometimes called, with your hat tipped back, listening to loud and insistent barkers call you into a shadowy tent for a show, was not only a distraction from viewing displays of seed corn but also a sign of serious moral decay.

Carnivals and barkers and amusement rides were, however, there to stay. The numbers demanded it. The agricultural society, like other prominent fair-givers across the country, derived a goodly amount of annual income from its arrangements with various amusement companies. The fair board shopped around, trying different companies every year. They made real efforts to provide Minnesota with clean entertainment, and efforts were probably also made to keep the Midway an honest operation. But the nature of the carnival beast was a flashy outside with a sassy inside. Some of those tents did hold scantily clad ladies; some of those games were tilted a bit, or more than a bit, in favor of the out-of-towner behind the counter. Then, as now, as it had been back into antiquity, the traveling carnival was a different world from the one its patrons inhabited.

The fair tried. In 1904, its managers promised "the tone will not be allowed to drop below the proper level." Nonetheless, it was going to be a good, "snappy" show, removed to an enclosure where the unsuspecting would not get an eyeful of some wayward Fatima doing her ballyhoo. But "when you visit a 'Pike,'" Minnesotans were reminded, "you don't have the idea you are going to a Sunday school picnic."

Whoever the contractor was, the Pike had always carried a merry-go-round along with its other attractions. The earliest on the grounds, an independently owned operation, appeared in 1892. Little is known about what kind of machines they were, or how elaborate. The merry-go-round was probably the most familiar of the rides and attractions on the Pike; it may have been placed close to the entrance to draw the cautious in. Or perhaps a little farther along the row; going in for a ride on the merry-go-round could provide a little glimpse of show fronts and barkers, even if one were properly horrified afterward. Wherever placed, the merry-go-rounds were consistently popular and always moneymakers. Everything on the pike was, or it didn't last.

After the 1913 fair, there occurred one of the periodic upheavals about the moral dangers of going over the Pike. In September, one Miss Agnes Peterson, representing the women's division of the state labor bureau, made a complaint to the state agricultural society "in regard to objectionable features in some of the shows on the grounds." The fair responded. "No More Midway at State

Fair," trumpeted one headline in the March 1914 *St. Paul Daily News*. "The old-fashioned nonsensical amusement carnival, such as has been shown . . . has 'played' the Minnesota State Fair for the last time." And "The fair board has decided to depart from the time-honored custom and put on an educational carnival, moral in nature." It would be, the fair announced, the "Wonderway," to be run by fair management itself and not let out to concessionaires.

The fair was not, however, willing to make the carnival entirely educational, giving up the receipts from all the amusement attractions that had been on the let-out Pike for all those years. The secretary himself, in his report to the governor in 1913, had acknowledged this: "We hardly believe that anyone would be so rash as to say that if the music and amusement features of the Fair were eliminated . . . the outside gate receipts would not show a very material decrease. I have heard good 'Fair' men place it as high as fifty per cent. Certainly, from ten to twenty per cent would be a most conservative estimate." The merry-go-round and a few other rides, while sometimes called frivolous, had never really been in question morally and were very popular.

In April 1914 there was a small announcement in the Friday evening *Minneapolis Journal* under the headline, "Fair Board Decides On New Amusements": "A roller coaster is to be a feature among amusements at the state fair grounds this year, and the fair board will install a big permanent merry-go-round. Action on both matters was taken at a meeting of the board of managers today. A contract was approved for erection of the roller coaster, which will be built at the rear of the grandstand."

Austin McFadden, a traveler, an entrepreneur, and a showman, had almost certainly visited the 1913 fair to assess its prospects as a site for the kind of permanent amusements he could profitably supply. That fall, the two independent merry-go-rounds had carried nearly thirty thousand riders, the Ocean Wave (something like today's scrambler), fifteen thousand, and the Ferris wheel, nearly nine thousand. The Minnesota State Fair was bustling, prosperous, and interested in permanent attractions that would not be associated with the sometimes-shady Pike. McFadden was willing and able to provide them.

It isn't known whether McFadden approached the fair or the fair approached McFadden. But, according to fair spokesman Jerry Hammer, "in 1914, Minnesota was the prestigious Fair. It was the biggest of them all; it was the undisputed best Fair. If McFadden was looking for an event at which to roll the dice with a short-term attraction, this was it."

In the big splash story of the *St. Paul Pioneer Press* on the Sunday before the Minnesota State Fair was to open in 1914, a hand-drawn headline trumpeted "Fun for State Fair Visitors," followed by "Amazing Stunts in the Air and on the Ground are Promised." Although the livestock and farm product displays were on the way to the fairgrounds, and hundreds of people from across the state were thinking anxiously or excitedly about their entries, the agricultural activities of the fair were not the focus of that day's release. The fair's promoters were concerned with trumpeting the less noble parts of the fair's ventures. The abolition of the

Pike and its pleasures had been well publicized, and some members of the public were doubtless pleased at the thought that there would be no harem girls or shady tent games available to tempt the populace. But there might also be a few potential patrons who were thinking the fair might be a little dull this year without the Pike. It was time for the fair's pressmen to lay that idea to rest. It was time for the ballyhoo.

"There will be many strange amusement features presented to the Northwest at the Minnesota State Fair this year," reported the *Pioneer Press*. "The big exposition has succeeded in engaging some of the highest priced acts in this country and abroad. Those in charge do not hesitate to term it the best bill of its kind ever presented at Hamline."

"At the head of the program," the paper went on, "as an object of interest, is Lincoln Beachey, the great little aviator. Seated at the tip of his aeroplane he glides, swoops, loops the loop or merely soars, as the whim seizes him. It makes one thrill with wonderment to see him far up in the air, thousands of feet above the earth, turning over and over in his machine, without fear of a single mishap." Powered flight was only eleven years old in 1914. Airplanes were a novelty and a thrill, but they were also a stirring glimpse into a technological future. It may be that Austin McFadden, the consummate promoter, watched Beachey and the fascinated audience from his attractions near the grandstand and decided on his traveling airplane tent exhibit during those few days in September. McFadden was not one to miss a trick, and the same people lining up for his roller coaster were streaming into the grandstand for a closer look at the airplane.

The action on the ground in 1914 was headlined by auto races on the fair's nationally famous mile-long dirt track. The greatest drivers of their day competed, including Louis Disbrow, Eddie Rickenbacker, and Barney Oldfield. The newspaper spread featured a photo of Oldfield dressed in a very natty jacket, clutching a cigar between his teeth and an apparently disembodied steering wheel in his hands. McFadden certainly went over to the grandstand to see the famous driver; Oldfield was later one of the drivers he sponsored in road races in Los Angeles. The fair advertised "a strenuous contest between the gasoline speed kings" and offered $1,500 in aggregate prizes for world's records.

Then as now, Americans liked speed and technology and any possible intersection between the two. No sooner was something invented than somebody began to race it; no opportunity should be missed. With aviator Beachey and the race car drivers both in Hamline, a race would be staged in an "attempt to determine the long disputed supremacy of earth and air craft." "Attempts" were an important part of the annual fair ballyhoo. It seemed that everyone was attempting something in 1914, and it must have been plenty of fun to watch.

A lot of those grand attempts were made in front of the grandstand crowd, an extremely busy place and, happily for McFadden with his brand-new carousel and roller coaster across the street, a huge traffic draw. Virtually all the big crowd-pleasers took place there. In addition to the relatively new mania for auto racing, there was a long-standing tradition of harness racing at the fair, and big purses were offered to attract both horsemen and fans. Over the five-day program, some $26,000 would be awarded. The horse race crowds would be additionally entertained by "an old-fashioned cross country fox hunt with hounds, horses, and horns."

Auto polo, a new enthusiasm, promised the crowd hazards, the roar of engines, and the possibility of accident. "Auto Polo," said the *Pioneer Press*, is "similar to pony polo, save that it is played in autos, and is far more dangerous." It had "created a sensation in the east. . . . As the machines turn turtle in nearly every game, or rush into each other while pursuing the ball, there is danger of injury or death at nearly every turn." Pony polo was not as dangerous (horses rarely turn turtle during the game, or if they do, they get right up), but it, too, had its novelty in 1914: "It is said that several women will appear in special games during the week."

There were parachute drops, elephants, and vaudeville and acrobatic troupes in the fair of 1914. There were suffragette movies shown on the Midway; they created "a real sensation." Minnesotans streamed in the gates to their own window on the world. There would be the annual concentration on agriculture, growing state industries, ladies handicrafts, and new farm implements. But the fair would also and always act as a concentrated glimpse of the rest of the world, with its inventions, its amusements, its burgeoning technologies, and its pleasures, not always agricultural. The Pike might be gone; having fun at the fair would never be.

The fun to be had at the former Midway received big play in the papers:

> One of the big amusement features of the Fair this
> year is to be The World at Home, a big educational

show staged on Wonderway, at the lip of the Lagoon. It will consist of a number of clean, high-class vaudeville attractions, some of which have never been staged before. . . . In another will be shown the Garden of Allah, presenting four score or more of persons from the Far East just as they live in their native land. There will be a menagerie of wild beasts and birds selected from one of the zoological parks of America. The other shows will be similar in nature. The World at Home is being widely advertised as a children's show.

Clearly there would be fun for adults as well; those "persons from the Far East" in the "Garden of Allah" sounded particularly promising.

The Panama Canal, which had opened the same year, was very big at the 1914 fair. In addition to a "gigantic" model on the Wonderway, the canal was the chief piece of scenery for the fair's annual fireworks pageant and spectacle. This grand performance, repeated nightly at the grandstand, was one of the most popular and enduring traditions of the fair. In earlier years, hundreds of people had staged spectacles such as "The Burning of Rome," with toppling scenery, smoke, and music. This year, the "spec" was entitled "The Opening of the Panama Canal," and it was packed with incident:

In the background will be a scenic picture of the Panama canal over 400 feet long. In this setting will be shown a portion of old Panama City, with its wharves, market places, churches and quaint architecture. Behind it, looming out in perspective, will be the great Spillway, Limon Bay, the towering mountains, Gatun lock and the Atlantic Ocean.

People from all the countries of the world will be represented on the stage, correctly costumed in gala attire. There will be 300 persons in the spectacle. Among them will be high officials of the United States, official dignitaries from other countries, soldiers and marines from all the nations, picturesque natives from South America, padres, friars, bull fighters, Japanese jinricksha men, crippled beggars, strolling musicians and Panama dancing girls.

At the end of the spectacle, a terrific detonation will be heard and the fireworks display will be opened. This is to represent the dynamiting of the last obstacle separating the Atlantic and Pacific Oceans. Due to the interest aroused over the opening of the Panama Canal, it is believed that the pyrotechnic display this year will be unusually popular.

Now *that* was entertainment. And all those entertained Minnesotans would be walking right by McFadden's sparkling new merry-go-round and coaster on their way to and from the often jam-packed grandstand. From morning until night, when the Atlantic and Pacific Oceans were being joined in fireworks and detonation, the corner of Commonwealth and Underwood was one of the best-traveled spots on the grounds.

McFadden would be heavily reliant on traffic and on the band organ and barkers to draw in the crowds. In this glittering array of publicity to entice visitors to come to the fair, the new permanent rides got very short shrift. After the one-sentence announcement in April of a roller coaster and a "big merry-go-round," there is no mention of McFadden's enterprises in the fair's collected press books. There was a story of a child who planned to exhibit a four-legged chicken, and a photo of an acrobatic troupe that performed in colonial wigs and breeches. But about the inaugural spin of McFadden's carousel, which would create a storm of publicity when it went up for sale seventy-five years later, there was nothing.

In every year, before and since, the fairgrounds were a beehive of activity in the weeks that precede the opening. McFadden was trying to erect his rides in the midst of a whirlwind, as hundreds of people prepared for the fair. Every bit of material that went into the construction of booths and displays—the lumber, the hardware, the paint, the decorative pieces—had to be trucked or teamed onto the grounds and assembled. New exhibits were created from the ground up, the responsibility of the exhibitor. Carpenters, electricians, painters, plumbers, and decorators in great numbers filled the grounds with the sounds of construction. The fair's own staff, the exhibitors and vendors themselves, professional craftsmen, and a great deal of what was called casual labor swarmed over a thousand projects, preparing for the descent of the public, their edification, and their cash.

Then, of course, the booths and display areas were filled with goods; constant delivery wagons filled the unpaved streets. The county exhibitors arrived in droves, with their bushels of prize corn and vegetables to be meticulously arranged in decorative swirls. Livestock arrived by train. Horses from nearby could be ridden in to their fair quarters. Scrubbed-up bulls and well-groomed sheep, brilliantly colored roosters and the more modest hens, huge sows and their offspring, all the live pageantry was brought, squealing and mooing and neighing, to its appointed place.

The spectacle would have been rehearsing at the grandstand ("places for all jinricksha men and crippled beggars, please!" they must have called), airplanes and race cars were arriving, and, of course, when the carnival company showed up to set up the new "educational" Wonder Way, there would have been the Panama Canal to get into place.

McFadden must have had his hands full. All the construction materials for the carousel building and its decoration and the roller coaster were brought in from off site, and crews were hired. Rail yards in 1914 ran directly into the fairgrounds, so the carousel equipment must have been off-loaded there and teamed over to the site of the new building. Local workmen had to be hired and local materials bought. We know that McFadden paid for roofing paper because, after the building was done, he thriftily sold the remainder to the fair; the fair in those days made public report of all transactions, no matter how small, but that is the only record of all that feverish activity.

A wooden roller coaster like the Cannonball would have taken thousands of board feet of lumber. National Amusement Park Historical Association historian Jim Futrell, examining pictures of the Cannonball, believes McFadden could have had virtually everything for the coaster fabricated locally, including the tracks: "I would estimate that the top of the lift hill was forty-five to fifty feet. The trains are three seats in each car, and two cars per train. So it looks like he's built a super-sized figure eight coaster. Primarily back then, their one concern was getting as many people on and off the ride as possible, because they were paying by the ride."

McFadden chose a simple and even old-fashioned technology for the Cannonball. The new under-friction coasters had been patented in 1912 but didn't really catch on until the twenties. The side-friction Cannonball, said Futrell, "was easy to build. They probably had all the engineering done on previous rides. And it was inexpensive to build, because it minimized engineering and engineering costs. It would be easier for him to get a return on his investment." It was compact, taking up less space on McFadden's rented plot of ground: "It's like three layers of track, so you can stack a lot of track on top of each other."

"They threw those things up real quick back then. They'd bring in a big labor crew and hammer it together in about a month," said Futrell. The Cannonball would have towered over everything in the vicinity except the grandstand; the workers on top of its fragile-looking structure and walking over its tracks would have had a grand view of the beehive below them as the fair was prepared.

There was one complicating factor equally true for everyone working on the grounds in late August 1914. "Rainy weather," said the St. Paul paper, "has interfered with the erection of booths and stands this week." Considerable fluctuation in Minnesota weather is entirely normal, and this mention probably indicates regular downpours. It must have been really damp up on that coaster track and really muddy at that new building site.

Any carousel is like a three-dimensional jigsaw puzzle, with thousands of parts. The Philadelphia Toboggan Company sent chief foreman Charles Bowditch to Minnesota for a full two weeks. Despite the essential simplicity of the machine, assembly could be a challenge and may have been complicated by the logistics of shipping. The motor, for example, was sent separately from the machine itself and probably arrived just in time for the opening. Even after it was put together, the merry-go-round needed a shakedown period to make sure that all was in order. With only six days of the fair to start making back his investment, McFadden would have wanted to be sure of his product.

But still, opening days do arrive, whatever the frenzy that precedes them.

And on Monday, September 7, 1914, PTC #33 opened for business for the first time. It began in the morning, as the first fairgoers were streaming through the turnstiles a few blocks away and starting their strolls down Commonwealth Avenue. The band organ began its loud call, which would bring in customers continuously for the next six days. Ticket takers were in place, perhaps a barker on the walk, maybe the sun even broke through the clouds. The "staff" would have been properly, and warmly, dressed in suits and hats, according to the fashion of the times. The mirrors and the brass poles were polished, and there was certainly a large sign that said "FIVE CENTS" and, perhaps, "RIDE THE GIANT CARROUSEL." The four-row machine was much larger than any of the traveling merry-go-rounds that had

187

been on the grounds before. The horses were brand spanking new, the band organ's dancing figures conducted their music in a stiff and ceremonious way, and no doubt the ticket takers had put on new collars for the occasion. McFadden may have thrown the clutch himself for the first ride. Bowditch was probably looking on. Certainly the "fog" bell clanged to warn the first riders to hold on. McFadden and Bowditch would not have waited for a full load of seventy-odd riders; the important thing was to get the carousel moving. Get the lights flashing, get the music blaring, get the people smiling and stopping. Get those nickels.

The crowds thickened, drawn by the band organ and the glitter of the grand new machine. A line of jostling families with excited children formed. The building filled up with people holding tickets. The carousel stopped and reloaded. And on the third or fourth ride, after only 135 tickets were sold, the main bearing shaft broke. The carousel would not turn again until late Wednesday night.

This was a terrible setback for McFadden's new Minnesota enterprise. There would be only a handful of riders on the first day and none at all on Tuesday or for most of Wednesday. The fair lasted only six days

The pressure was on; #33 was brand new, and it was down. Patrons were walking by the carousel, unable to spend their nickel there and perfectly willing to spend it elsewhere.

The surviving admission numbers indicate that the competition cleaned up, particularly on the opening day. The five-cent merry-go-round associated with the Wonder Way carried 8,603 riders on Monday, nearly five times as many as any other day of its run. On Tuesday and Wednesday, despite continuing cold weather, heavy patronage of that merry-go-round continued, while McFadden and Bowditch struggled with repairs on their big, brand-new, broken machine.

This may have been the time when foreman Bowditch's own accounts record several night letters to the company and expenses for repairs. Later in the year, PTC would pay McFadden $73.20 marked "erection and repairs during September 1914." The fair was going on without the carousel, and it wouldn't be back for another full year.

It may have been a comfort to McFadden that his Cannonball coaster was a success from the very first. The opening day admission, at ten cents, was just over fifteen thousand, an astonishing total and by far the heaviest patronage of any percentage attraction on the grounds. The coaster would remain hugely popular throughout the week and end up with a paid admission of 58,004. The outside gate admission for the entire run of the fair was only 322,000; the coaster was a huge success. And the customers were riding in spite of the rain and cold, which continued to plague both fairgoers and concessionaires. "The cool days, and especially the cool evenings, made the visitor quite uncomfortable without winter wraps," reported the secretary's annual summary. "The weather was so cold that the sale of ice fell off 60% from the 1913 Fair."

Late Wednesday night, the carousel began to turn again and people began to flow in, as they would in steadily increasing numbers for the remainder of the fair. The ticket takers squeezed in 1,355 people after repairs were complete on dnesday ("Rain and extremely cold"); if they were running reasonably full, that would be under twenty rides. The numbers got better. On Thursday ("Rain practically all day. Very cold"), just over three thousand. On Friday ("Dark. Cloudy up to eleven o'clock. Very Cold"), just over five thousand. On Saturday, closing day, the weather finally turned for the better, and patrons poured through the gates. At the next-door grandstand, an enormous crowd watched as a new world record, a new state record, and a new motorcycle speed record were set: "Lincoln Beachey, King of the Air, looped the loop at 6,000 feet altitude, flew upside down and raced his plane against Barney Oldfield's car five times around the track."

Just to the east, 7,417 riders paid admission to the big new carousel. The competition, the merry-go-round, was left in the dust on Saturday, with only 1,420 riders. The week's total for #33 was just over seventeen thousand riders. If the carousel had run properly throughout, McFadden would surely have had the two most heavily patronized percentage attractions on the grounds that year. He already had the most advantageous percentage deal at 15 percent. The World at Home Shows, Inc., paid 27 percent to the fair, and even the baby incubator was at 25 percent. The coaster and carousel looked to be profitable ventures for both McFadden and the fair.

On September 7, after barely four days of complete operation for the carousel, the ballyhoo of 1914 fair week was over. It was time to shut down.

Then as now, the fair closed up fairly quickly. All the exhibitors, with their livestock and their goods, streamed off the grounds and headed for home, taking down their displays and picking up their premiums as they went. The vendors, even faster, may have had another venue waiting for their candy floss or their bags of peanuts. And the noisy throng of the public, with the exception of the few children who always hang about watching everything go away, disappeared in an instant. When the grandstand show was over on Saturday night, with the Atlantic and Pacific joined in fireworks for the last time, the lights went off. The next morning, all that was left were street sweepers, a few laggards who slept in, and a great many people packing up.

McFadden probably didn't have too much to do to close down his amusements. This carousel wasn't going anywhere. The horses may have been taken down from their brass poles for storage (the original packing boxes were still on the fairgrounds as late as 1939), but they would certainly have remained in the carousel building. The massive simplicity of the carousel mechanism made it all simple. Turn it off. Cover the band organ against dirt and mice. Close the door.

The carousel would not be touched again until the next summer, establishing a pattern that would not be changed for the next seventy-five years. Outside the shuttered building, fall arrived. The magnificent oaks and maples that covered the fairgrounds were red and gold in the slanted yellow sun. The carousel slept. The harsh Minnesota winter drifted snow high up on the doors. Spring would arrive. Summer would come and pass. Along about the middle of August, someone would come and unlock the padlock and open the door. After a little preparation, a little grease, a little brass polish, all in a flash, the ballyhoo again. The throng returns, and the carousel turns again.

(1989, 2019)

Verse VI

THIS I BELIEVE

This I Believe

A speech delivered in a spiritual community. I don't take many assignments, but I took this one.

I have struggled with this. I have avoided it like poison. Like the plague. I agreed to do it almost a year ago, when it was safely distant, and I remember thinking, *it's your turn, Peg*. I am very big on taking my turn. So I spent January in a light state of dread and February in a kind of periodic paralysis, drafting, stopping, drafting, stopping.

Should I take the biographical approach? The confessional approach? The "hail fellow traveler well met" approach? The literary approach, where I mostly quote other people about what I believe?

In drafting, which is part of the work of the writer, even typing the words "This I Believe" in caps seemed overly declarative.

It isn't that I don't believe in anything. Quite the contrary.

It might be that what I believe in is unfashionable.

It might be that I had to learn what to believe, not having been taught to believe in much in a perilous childhood. This gives one, or at least it gave me, a highly and possibly overdeveloped sense of privacy.

But what I think I discovered in the drafting is that I believe in too many things. At least too many things for one piece of writing and speaking.

Yet, here I am. It was my turn. Plus, thinking about the things you believe in is hardly wasted time. And discovering you believe in too many things for one writing is a rather happy complaint. And it's appropriate to talk about these things in this room, privacy notwithstanding, because this is where a large part of my learning in these matters has been formed. It turned out that, while I thought I was coming to this community for the intellectual life, it's been my spiritual life, a phrase that once made me shudder, that was revived and discovered here.

Church was a social accessory when I was a child. The parish this and the parish that. The parental cocktail parties were glittery, and none of what looked like friendships and relationships were what I would now call close. But you grow up where you are. I was a romantic and drawn to beauty, and for that reason I was drawn to church. I loved the ritual and the anthemic stories. I loved the color of the vestments and the height of the church and the serenity of the statuary. I loved the quiet. At the age of eleven, I was the organist for 7:30 Mass, still then the Latin Mass, and I remember the pleasure of entering the empty church and sitting alone in the loft, separate from the few early risers below. I loved the familiarity and the sense of history. I liked mumbling the responses. I knew they were part of something much bigger than the small, hard world of my family. And then, as soon as I went away to college, I stopped.

My heart opened—I felt it open—on the delivery table when my firstborn was placed in my arms, leaving an inky footprint on my belly. I made a surprised sound, and the doctor, busy with something in my nether regions, asked if

I'd felt pain, a patently foolish question. But what I'd grunted at was a physical sensation in my chest. Lying on the table, I felt something in my heart that had been closed—doors?—fly open, and all my love rushed out toward my child. Once those doors fly open, they never close again. All that rushing, pouring out: love and fear and joy. And, it turned out, the ability to believe in things larger than the rush of my own days.

Once a number of years ago I was invited to join a book club that was largely populated by high-powered media women. It was called book club although there was little book conversation. I shortly, open-mouthed with astonishment at the way they talked about the world, developed a more descriptive name for it that involved alliteration with the word *book*, and also included the words *wine* and *whine*. I enjoyed the fast talk and the hard edge in that crowd, and there were twelve members, so you only had to entertain them once a year. I am in many ways a deliberate innocent, though, so when it came time for me to suggest a book, I suggested one that I really loved. Fiction, which is not common for me. The book discussion, never a lengthy or substantive affair, was even shorter that night, and finally one of the women asked me with a rather puzzled air what I liked about this book.

My answer was unexpected, even to me. "What I like about this book," I said suddenly, "is that it is about things that I believe in." "What," someone asked without interest, "were those?" And I spouted, "Courage. Wonder. Honor. Invention. The power of evil and the power of good to triumph over it. The essential and enduring beauty of the world. The deep pulse of the city. The wild winter landscape. Magic."

I assure you, that stopped the conversation dead in its tracks. And a couple of months later, it was my turn to entertain, and right after that I became "too busy" to remain a member of that particular book club.

I was surprised in retrospect that I spoke so truly in that room, and maybe I wouldn't have if I'd thought a little more before speaking. But it seemed like an orderly and necessary thing to do, to respond with truth when asked what you believe. To answer falsely, or dismissively, would have seemed like a spoiling. Although it was well before I came to carry this idea in my bones, as I do now, I was not hiding or pretending or being anyone other than who I am.

When I was drafting this speech, for a while I went through a simple listing, and that seemed like a way in to the Big Question of what a person believes.

I believe in music. And its power to illuminate and transform. Me, and everyone else. Particularly when we are making music together. And especially when it's gospel and roots music.

I believe in church architecture.

I believe in the precision and power of words.

I believe in the necessity of staying awake in the world.

I believe in biology, that we are creatures whose oversized and sometimes overbusy brains encourage us to disallow and forget the fact that we are flesh and blood, the product of an evolutionary process that seems very important to us and is in fact only a tiny, tiny slice of the universe at large.

I believe that what would unite this world fastest, what would make everyone instantly forget their differences, would be a good old-fashioned, thumping, hostile alien invasion from the stars. We'd be bonded *then*.

I believe in my children. And in your children. They really are an arrow that we shoot into a future that we will never see. Lean back and let go and let that arrow fly.

I believe in the power of artifacts, things we can hold in our hands from the past, our historic past and our own past, and I believe that these things carry a distinct charge, like an electrical charge, that can be felt and examined.

I believe that if we look over the landscape, and squint to throw our eyes out of focus, and open up all our pores and listen that we can glimpse everything that has happened there in the past. Our ancestors, familial and species, moving over the land, going about their vanished business, rising up, falling down, vanishing. But not gone.

I believe in beauty. And in the imperative of seeing beauty in every day.

I believe in the power of story. To teach. And to make teachings stick.

It got be a long list in my draft, the Things I Believe.

Sacred music. Cathedral architecture. Essential justice. The power of the sky. The necessity of silence in order to be able to hear. Accepting uncertainty and learning to be able to say "I don't know," when all my training taught against that. Things happening for a purpose, and people appearing in one's life for a purpose. And how bread has to rise.

Singing all the verses. And singing them in the middle; as an alto, I always seek the middle harmony, the one that fills out the chord.

I have been in this community for a long time. I first walked in the door on a Sunday morning, alone, and I came because I had moved out of my busy city life with my husband and two small children. I had been completely and happily bound up in my work for years. There is nothing so immersive as the theater. Sometimes whole seasons would go by without my giving notice to the outside world. Or wait: there is nothing so immersive as being a mother to small children. Sometimes whole seasons would go by. Every day I was left alone with my two small children on our hobby farm. And although this was a choice we had made together, after some months, I was in desperate need of adult conversation and a reminder of what had once been my intellectual life. I found it here. And, in due course, my children found a home and a like-thinking community here. They did much of their growing here, through religious education, through the teen group, through sex education where they learned to practice putting a condom on a banana, through the youth conventions, through being youth representatives on our church board, with an equal voice in discussion and contemplation. Young adults now, they are UU through and through. Not regularly churched, but thoroughgoing free thinkers with a highly developed moral sense. They are still in touch with many of the young people they grew up with here. They are still welcomed when they come through the door at the holidays. My husband started coming when our toddler daughter refused to go to Sunday class without a parent and I refused to give up my hour in the adult meeting room. In time, he, too, became embedded here.

Some of the things I believe I have learned in this community. I have come to believe strongly that it is best to say what you think and to try to speak and act honorably in all things. I have come to believe that spending time in a community that says that out loud and regularly may be the best way to make that a norm. I have come to believe that Sunday is a Sabbath and that I need a Sabbath. I have come to believe that every time I feel most alone and isolated, most like the outlier, the stranger, if I raise my eyes and look around, I will see that there are people all around me who are engaged in the same struggles and uncertainties that I feel. We are all on the very same continuum. We have much more in common than we have separating us.

And every time I am privileged to stand in this pulpit and look out there, I take strength from the beauty of the faces I see, each one very different, each in our own places on that continuum, and each one entirely the same in desire to open and to act for good in the world, each in our own way. I like to look around the room when the opening words are being spoken and find a child who is speaking them by rote and watch those shining faces say, "love is the spirit of this church, and service is its law. This is our great covenant, to dwell together in peace, to seek the truth in understanding, and help one another."

There are people in this congregation, some of them in this room, to whom I can turn for a moment of comfort. With whom I can freely howl with laughter in a most undignified way. With whom I can exchange a glance of understanding when something beautiful or moving passes through the room. Brothers and sisters. Siblings separated at birth. I have found here no need to "hide, to pretend, or to be anything other than who I am." And the speaking of those words, every week, has become a powerful incantation that has replaced the rituals and ceremonies of my childhood church. I have found here the wit to recognize that I am a better person and have a chance at making a better world if I behave the same way outside this room. If I go through my days without hiding, without pretending, without being anything other than who I am and who I am called to be.

I'm not sure that, without this community, I would have ever noticed that as a value. I'm not sure I would have waked up to that shattering observation.

So: Beauty. Gratitude. The pleasure and nourishment of sitting in a circle that is giving serious consideration to the world.

And oh, yes: Divinity. I think the most that I can say about that is that it does not seem to me that the music of Bach, and the architecture of cathedrals, and the immense beauty and order of the natural world, and the tremendous surging power of singing together—it does not seem to me that those things can mean nothing, and it does not seem likely that they are accidental.

I am afflicted by clippings. I am a looker, a seeker after kindred spirits, and often I find them in other times and places, or maybe I can just recognize them better when they are distilled into a book or a poem or a quote.

I have clippings so yellowed that they are brown.

"We live only to discover beauty. All else is a form of waiting." Kahlil Gibran.

"Writing is very easy. All you do is sit at the typewriter until little drops of blood appear on your forehead." Red Smith.

Poems innumerable.

Speeches from Shakespeare, which I carry in my head.

And this from Edith Wharton: "In spite of illness, in spite of the archenemy, sorrow, one can remain alive long past the usual date of disintegration if one is unafraid of change, insatiable in intellectual curiosity, interested in big things, and happy in small ways."

This I Believe.

(2013)

ABOUT THE AUTHOR

Peg Guilfoyle is a born-and-bred Midwesterner, who has been writing since a young age, with her commentary and features seen in many newspapers and magazines. Her regional history books include *The Guthrie Theater: Images, History, and Inside Stories* (Nodin Press, Midwest Book Award) and *The Basilica of Saint Mary: Voices From A Landmark*. Peg Projects, Inc., has produced organizational history books for private and corporate clients, with numerous awards, including the Minnesota Book Award. Peg has written two volumes of a projected trilogy on history and genealogy. She has been production manager and stage manager at many regional theaters, including ten years at the Guthrie Theater, and served as Producing Director for Theatre and Dance at the University of Minnesota. Her arts vocabulary is wide-ranging; she has managed residency programs in many arts disciplines and communities, and is an accomplished speaker. Peg has served as project manager for various promotional and planning efforts. She is an active volunteer and board leader in various organizations around the Twin Cities of Minneapolis and St. Paul, and is widely involved in citizen activism. She is the mother of two, and grandmother of two. This is her first book of essays.

Like this book?

How to Order More

Singing All The Verses: Essays From A Mid-American

available at **amazon.com**

(Kind words posted on amazon always appreciated!)

Or order direct from the author at **pegguilfoyle.com**

Signed and inscribed copies,
personalized and mailed direct to you

inquiries for speaking engagements and book clubs

book consultations

books on commission for private and corporate clients

$19.95 plus $7 shipping

(first class USPS in United States, international by arrangement)

(Paypal, or other method by arrangement)

Peg Guilfoyle | Peg Projects, Inc. pegguilfoyle.com

Made in the USA
Monee, IL
10 August 2020